P9-BYV-457

Nine Minutes on Monday

The Quick and Easy Way
to Go from Manager to Leader

JAMES ROBBINS

New York   Chicago   San Francisco   Lisbon   London   Madrid   Mexico City
Milan   New Delhi   San Juan   Seoul   Singapore   Sydney   Toronto

To my wife, Kelly.
Without you, I am less than I am.

The **McGraw·Hill** Companies

Copyright © 2013 by James Robbins. All rights reserved. Printed in the United States of America. Except as permitted under the United States Copyright Act of 1976, no part of this publication may be reproduced or distributed in any form or by any means, or stored in a data base or retrieval system, without the prior written permission of the publisher.

7 8 9 0 DOC/DOC 1 8 7 6 5

ISBN 978-0-07-180198-0
MHID 0-07-180198-7

e-ISBN 978-0-07-180199-7
e-MHID 0-07-180199-5

McGraw-Hill books are available at special quantity discounts to use as premiums and sales promotions or for use in corporate training programs. To contact a representative, please e-mail us at bulksales@mcgraw-hill.com.

Library of Congress Cataloging-in-Publication Data

Robbins, James.
  Nine minutes on Monday : the quick and easy way to go from manager to leader / by James Robbins.
    p. cm.
  Includes bibliographical references.
  ISBN 978-0-07-180198-0 (alk. paper) — ISBN 0-07-180198-7 (alk. paper) 1. Leadership. 2. Employee motivation. 3. Management. I. Title.
  HD57.7.J354 2012
  658.4'092—dc23

                                                    2012016224

Contents

Introduction
Never Turn Down a Man Who Wants to Be Sprayed

I will never forget the irate golfer who stood only a few feet away from me, screaming and daring me to spray him with water. I was a 17-year-old golf course worker who had been asked by my boss to drive around and manually water the greens at the Highwood Golf and Country Club because our irrigation system was not working. It was actually a pretty sweet assignment on a hot August day, driving from hole to hole in the water truck that had the power to shoot a stream of water a good 30 to 40 feet. It was on the fourteenth green where the showdown took place. I remember a foursome of gentlemen approaching the green and preparing to line up their putts, a sign for me to stop watering. It was during the moment that I was turning off the water and walking back to the truck that I accidentally spilled some water on one of the gentlemen's golf bags. The only reason I found this out was that one of the golfers yelled at me and approached with a furious look on his face.

"You got water on my bag!" he yelled. A bit surprised, I did what most 17-year-old kids would do who work at the golf course. I apologized sincerely, mentioning I had not seen it and promising that it wouldn't happen again. Apparently, my apology was not good enough for Mr. pink polo shirt golfer man because he continued to stand there right in my face pouring out vitriol that could only come from 13 bad holes of golf.

I had been raised well and taught the values of respect and humility, so it was fairly natural to apologize once again. After all, back then the customer was always right. My apology, although sincere, only seemed to irritate the man further, because the next thing I knew he was ranting and raving at me and daring me to spray all the bags. I distinctly remember him yelling, "Just get *all* the bags wet!"

I don't care what golf course you belong to, such behavior is bound to draw attention. In addition to Mr. Angry Golfer's three friends who were looking on in stunned and somewhat embarrassed silence, we now had an audience on the twelfth green and another at the fifteenth tee box which was only a few feet away. It was like a scene out of middle school, and I was just waiting for someone to start yelling, "Fight, fight, fight."

I was raised a good country kid, but I must confess that I only have so much humble in me. Mr. Angry Golfer man had pushed me to my limit. As he continued to dare me to spray the rest of the golf bags, I looked at him, still holding the large water hose in my hand, and said calmly, "Maybe I should spray you."

Do you remember the cartoons where Bugs Bunny and Elmer Fudd were engaged in all-out war, and there was always a moment where Elmer Fudd would flip out—his face would go red, steam would come out of his ears, and his eyes would turn all bloodshot? Well, that is what happened here. The golf guy freaked.

"What!!! Spray me, spray me. C'mon, I dare you. Spray me!"

As he went into a frenzied arm-waving tantrum, I tuned out for a moment and imagined what the next few minutes might look like. *"All I have to do is turn the nozzle on this hose and water will come rocket-*

ing out from the truck. It's probably going to knock him over, send him sprawling across the freshly cut golf green, covering his lovely pink polo shirt with grass clippings. He's probably going to charge at me, and there will most certainly be a fight. I'm going to get fired, but this just might be worth it."

But then I thought about college and how I needed this job to pay for my education. With that, I snapped out of my daydream and in reply to his demands that I spray him I said simply, "No, because I am not a jerk like you," and I walked away.

To this day I regret that!

In hindsight, I probably did the right thing, but wouldn't it have been a great story if I had sprayed him as he requested. It's funny how in life most of the regrets people have come from things they didn't do, chances they didn't take, or risks they shied away from. I also remember how only a few years later, while going to college, someone invited me to a leadership meeting at a local church I was attending. To be honest, I didn't know the first thing about leadership and didn't even know if it was something I could do. I agreed to come to the meeting, not knowing that I was about to embark on a lifelong journey of learning how to lead others. In fact, it is a journey I am still on today.

Leadership has to be one of the most difficult, at times frustrating, yet rewarding and fulfilling roles a person can have in life. I sincerely believe that leadership is not only a privilege, but one of the highest callings a person can have. Whether you are leading a country, a company, or two employees in the mailroom, the chance to motivate, inspire, direct, and serve others is truly thrilling. Leadership is a journey and one that requires consistent attention in order to avoid stagnation. With the demands on managers today, it is imperative that we continue to evolve, improve, and reinvent ourselves. This usually involves living outside our comfort zone for long stretches at a time. There have been moments in my life when I have found myself slipping into a safe and predictable routine—where my leadership seemed to be on autopilot. Looking back, these are the times with the fewest memories, the smallest amount of growth, and most certainly the times of little impact. There is too much at stake to take the position of leadership lightly. If you set your sights on becoming a great influencer of men and women—though the journey will be difficult—you will find the experience to be immensely rewarding, and I know you will have no regrets.

I am not sure what brought you to *Nine Minutes on Monday,* but I hope that within these pages you find not only inspiration but practical ideas that will help you lead your people to greater heights. If you take the principles from this book and use them to impact even one of your employees, then it will have served its purpose. Writing a book, as I have discovered, is hard work. But if this helps you in your leadership journey, then I'll be able to look back and know that the effort was worth the trouble, and with confidence say, "I have no regrets."

Enjoy.

PART I

The Three Truths

Why Mountain Climbers Make Lousy Mountain Guides

The task of the leader is to get his people from where they are to where they have not been.

—Henry Kissinger

The meeting lasted only a few minutes. When you are perched on the side of a mountain at 20,000 feet above sea level, it's not a good idea to sit around. We had been steadily making our way up the southwest side of Mt. Sajama, the highest peak in Bolivia and one of the highest in the western hemisphere. We still had over 1,500 vertical feet to go before reaching the summit, and it was almost noon. As tired as we were, it looked like this was as high as we would get. Osvaldo, our guide, radioed base camp, informing the people there that we had stopped in order to make a decision. The choices were simple—continue on toward the summit or abandon our attempt to reach the summit and retreat. The entire expedition to climb Mt. Sajama now rested in the hands of our leader.

We had been in Bolivia for nearly three weeks, climbing and acclimating to get ready for our attempt at Sajama. That morning at 2:30 a.m. we left high camp at 18,000 feet under the cover of darkness. There were five of us roped together, moving slowly under the lights of our headlamps, ever upward toward the glacier. Before sunrise, Jack, one of our team members, was having difficulty. After being assessed by our lead guide, John, the decision was made to take Jack back down to base camp. With our lead guide now departing for base camp with Jack in tow, there were just three of us left to go for the summit—Jim, a 33-year-old from North Carolina, Osvaldo, a Bolivian climbing guide who now took over for John, and me.

As we made our way up and onto the snow pack, the ground was littered with penitente, a type of snow formation common in South America that resembled pinnacles stretching up toward the sky. Our steel crampons chewed into the snow and ice as we made painstakingly slow progress toward a summit we could not see. Climbing at such altitudes can take a toll on your body, and just after sunrise Jim was beginning to feel the effects as he labored to continue. I could tell that Jim was getting tired as he stopped repeatedly and made comments about how hard this was.

The mountain was beginning to wear Jim down by slowly stripping away his will. The problem for Jim and me, however, was that we were down to our last guide and our last length of rope. If Jim quit now, we would all have to turn back; our quest for the summit would be over. Jim knew this and did his best to continue, but I began to doubt that he would last. What Jim needed now was motivation. What he could have really used was a motivational speaker climbing right behind him. Unfortunately, all he had was me, but, hey, I knew what to do. For the next hour I continued to spur Jim on with words of encouragement, looking for anything that would keep him going.

Then, sometime around mid-morning, something happened. It felt as if someone had sneaked up behind me and pulled my plug, draining away all my energy. My legs felt like heavy tree trunks, and an over-whelming feeling of fatigue washed over me. Because of a problem with our stove earlier in the day, we had limited water, and by not drinking enough, our bodies were beginning to feel the effects of dehydration. It was not long before I began to question my own ability to reach the summit. Soon my doubts began to erode my desire to reach the top as my aching body redirected my thoughts to the down-filled sleeping bag awaiting me in base camp. My desires were no longer to conquer the mountain, but to end this agony.

Now I had a problem. If I called it quits, it was over for all of us. I would be the cause of the failed expedition. It even crossed my mind that this story might not make a very good speech. As I searched for a way to escape my situation, a brilliantly creative and innovative solution came to me. As has been said, necessity is the mother of all invention.

"I don't need to quit!" I reasoned to myself, thinking with a brain a bit short on oxygen. "I just need *Jim* to quit." Because if Jim quit, I could too. It would be like an honorable discharge from the mountain. I could still go home and tell all my friends that I would have made the top if it was not for this other guy. I also believed I could outlast him because I was in very good shape at the time. So my encouraging words to keep Jim going began to be fewer and farther apart. After all, I surely didn't want to motivate him. However, I knew that Jim realized what was at stake and did not want to let me down. I knew what he was thinking and—I am ashamed to say this now, but I did something terrible—I opened the door a bit wider for Jim. I decided that, during one of our short rests, I would give Jim permission to quit. I would say to him, "Listen if you need to go down, that's OK with me."

I think Osvaldo sensed what was going on, which is why he decided to stop and call a meeting. Over the hours our pace had slowed, our attitudes had deteriorated, and I think both Jim and I wanted to give up, but neither of us wanted to be the first to suggest it. With crampons dug into the snow to keep from sliding down the mountain, Osvaldo got on the radio and, in his thick Bolivian accent, sent a transmission to base camp.

"Base camp, clients are tired. We are going to decide what to do next, whether to continue on or turn around and head back to base camp."

There we sat, the Atacama desert a few thousand feet below, with only the sound of a light wind teasing the mountain. Vince Lombardi, legendary football coach, once said, "Fatigue makes cowards of us all." Indeed, there we were, convinced we had reached our limit and longing for the home fires of base camp. The mountain demanded more than we could give, and now the fate of our expedition lay in the hands of Osvaldo, our leader. If we were to continue upward, it would require something extraordinary from him.

How do you get others to do something they feel they cannot do? How do you motivate people to do more, and be more, when they believe they are at their limit? Is motivation something we can *do* to people, or does it need to come from within the person themselves? Before we dive into these questions, let's first consider another. What was Osvaldo paid to do?

HOW CLIMBERS BECOME GUIDES

Before he became a mountain guide, Osvaldo was a talented climber in his own right. Who would entrust their life on a mountain at high altitude to someone who was not competent to lead them? Certainly not I. When Osvaldo was merely a climber, things were much simpler. As a mountaineer, he simply climbed mountains. Getting to the top was the only goal, and, as his skills improved, so too did the number of summits he reached. Success was easily defined—getting to the top and returning home safely to tell about it, while having some fun along the way. For Osvaldo, the mountain itself was the challenge to overcome and the focal point of his energy and attention. Over time, his climbing skills impressed someone enough that this person suggested he consider becoming a mountain guide. Instead of simply climbing mountains, why not get paid to help other people climb mountains? This is the mountaineering world's equivalent of frontline management.

While this is a natural evolution for a good climber like Osvaldo, it requires a monumental shift in his thinking. For Osvaldo, becoming a guide meant that the mountain was no longer the focal point of his energy and attention. Reaching the summit was now a by-product of how well he managed his new job—moving people. Osvaldo's experience as a mountain climber would serve him well in his new role. Because of his own path, he could relate to the demands of the mountains and their effects on people's minds and bodies. This experience alone would not make him a great mountain guide because mountain guides don't climb mountains; they help others to climb mountains.

So let's return to the question. What is Osvaldo paid to do?

If you ask a group of people, you will get a variety of answers, such as to keep us safe, to motivate us, and to make the trip enjoyable. While all these are important—especially the part about safety (just ask my mother)—in Osvaldo's mind, he is ultimately paid for one thing—to get people to the top of the mountain. And while there are parameters he must operate within, such as safety and enjoyment for the client, success for a mountain guide is primarily defined by getting people to the top and then getting them back down.

In fact, getting people to the top is a bit like his scoreboard. It is ultimately what he gets paid to do and what determines his success. After all, do you want to climb with a guide who has never managed to lead anyone to the top or, worse yet, one who has never returned anyone safely home? If Osvaldo's success is primarily based on whether or not his clients reach the summit, who is more important in the equation? Osvaldo? Or the clients? If you guessed the clients, you have answered correctly, because although Osvaldo is an impressive climber on his own, he has not been hired to climb mountains; he has been hired to help others climb mountains.

Let's leave the mountains for a moment and enter your workplace. As a manager, you undoubtedly have a full plate that is constantly spilling over with a seemingly endless list of to-do's. The million-dollar question, however, is what are you being paid to do? The secret to being a great manager lies in answering this question correctly. Great managers must make the same monumental shift that our friend Osvaldo had to make when he transitioned from mountaineer to climbing guide.

WHAT ARE YOU PAID TO DO?

Your primary job is to produce results, whatever they may be. Before you were a manager, you were also paid to produce results, but things were different then. Your focus was primarily on a set of tasks that over time produced a certain result. As a manager you are still paid to produce results, except that now it isn't really you who produces them; it's your people. The monumental shift required is moving from climbing mountains yourself to helping others climb mountains. As a manager you are paid to produce results through people, and because your success hinges on these results produced by the people you lead, you want to do everything in your power to help them be as successful as they can be.

As we sat at 20,000 feet, tired, dehydrated, and wanting to quit, Osvaldo could not afford to be just a mountain climber. What we needed was a mountain guide, a leader. With our summit bid in jeopardy, he had to figure out how to move and motivate us—to rally what we did have and apply it to the challenge at hand—Mt. Sajama's summit.

Leadership is the art and science of moving people. Whatever had taken us to 20,000 feet was not going to be enough to get us to the 21,463-foot roof of Bolivia. More would be needed from us. But since we believed that we were at our vertical limit, going farther rested on great leadership from a mountain guide who had once been a climber himself.

That's what this book is all about. How do you as a manager get your people to be the best they can be so that they get to the top of the mountain you're climbing? In addition, how do you accomplish this so that they have such an enjoyable journey they want to do it all over again with you guiding the way? Last, how do you accomplish all this in a challenging environment where your schedule is already insanely busy, as if someone has set the speed of your treadmill a few miles an hour faster than you can manage? In this new economy, managers around the world are pressed to find answers to these questions. Over the course of this book, you will learn a simple system to help you bring out the best in your employees, enabling them to produce results without adding hours worth of tasks to your plate. The nine principles found in this book will ignite the engagement, motivation, morale, and trust among your team members and will result in greater efficiency and higher levels of productivity.

Before we dive into these nine principles, I want first to introduce you to an invisible force that works in your favor to magnify your influence among your direct reports. Once you understand how this deeply ingrained psychological principle works, you will be even more motivated to devote yourself to excellence as a leader.

LEADERSHIP TRUTH 1

Mountaineers climb mountains.

Climbing guides help people climb mountains.

TRANSLATION

You are paid to produce results.

These results are created by the people you lead.

Therefore, your job is to help your people be as successful as they need to be in order to produce results.

Why Good People Will Obey Bad Orders

It is for each of us freely to choose whom we shall serve,
and find in that obedience our freedom.

—Mary Richards

On May 11, 1996, eight climbers died on the upper section of Mt. Everest after being caught in a terrible storm. Many factors contributed to the tragedy that day; one of them was that the climbing guides had failed to stick to their turnaround times, an error that left people too high on the mountain too late in the day. When you climb a mountain like Everest, you leave high camp at around midnight, and make your way through the dark along the summit ridge, hoping to get to the summit by mid- to late morning. Expedition guides set hard turn-around times. A turnaround time is simply the latest possible time at which you can still be heading up the mountain. Once you reach that point, no matter where you are, you need to start making your way back down the mountain. The turnaround time is supposed to be set in stone. If yours is 11:00 a.m., wherever you happen to be at 11:00 a.m., you had better be turning around and heading back down. There are countless stories of individuals who were just a few hundred feet from the summit and, because they had reached their turnaround time, had to abandon their summit dreams along with the $40,000 they paid just to take their shot. You can see how an expedition guide could potentially be an unpopular person in such situations, but with lives at stake, someone has to be the law.

On Everest that fateful day in May, some of the guides failed to enforce their turnaround times, and their clients ended up getting caught in a brutal storm that claimed nine lives and left others, like Texas doctor Beck Weathers, with severe and debilitating frostbite. While tragedies of this magnitude are rare, this one could have been minimized had the guides exercised their authority and, regardless of how unpopular the decision may have been, turned people around earlier. The sad reality is that the clients would have obeyed and would have had a much better chance of reaching the safety of high camp before the storm hit. On the mountain, the mountain guide has the loudest voice.

What if I told you that you were the most important person in your organization? You probably would not believe me, and for good reason, because it's probably not true. While you may not be the most influential person in your entire organization, you are the most influential among a very important group of people—your direct reports. This may be hard to swallow, but accepting it is key to your effectiveness. More than anyone else in your organization, no one has the potential to impact your direct reports as much as you do. The CEO, CFO, COO or president of the board may have a lot of organizational power, but day in and day out, the person with the most weight in the work lives of your direct reports is you. Because of some deep social conditioning, an invisible force exists that lends weight to your words and actions. This force finds its power in a principle I call *weighted relationships*.

INFLICTING PAIN ON THE INNOCENT

Leonard Bickman conducted an interesting study on the affect of authority and obedience. In this experiment, Bickman had a person stop pedestrians in the street and say, "Hey, you see that guy over there by the parking meter? He's overparked but doesn't have any change. Give him a dime." Then the requester would turn and walk away. Bickman repeated the study again, only this time the same man telling people to give the man a dime was dressed in a security guard's uniform.

The results were surprising; 42 percent of people complied with the plain-clothed man, while a whopping 92 percent complied when the request came from the same man dressed as a security guard.

In 1955 a psychologist named Stanley Milgram ran an interesting experiment. I want you to imagine for a moment that it's 1955 and you have volunteered for his study. You are taken into a room to meet your partner (another volunteer). You are told that you will be paid for this experiment and that you will assume the role of the teacher, while the other volunteer will be the student. You will be in separate rooms and must communicate by intercom only. You will ask the other volunteer questions, and for every answer he gets wrong, you will administer an electric shock to him through a complicated-looking machine connected to electrodes attached to his arm. (All of us probably have someone in mind whom we would love to be paired up with to do this experiment, but let's not go down that road.)

The "shock machine" that is in front of you has a series of buttons. Pushing them in order successively increases the electrical charge incrementally, starting at 15 volts and maxing out at a whopping 450 volts of electricity. With each wrong answer, you are required to increase the voltage of the shock administered.

As you take your place in front of the machine, the only other person in the room with you is a researcher dressed in a white lab coat. The experiment goes smoothly at first, but as soon as your partner answers one of the questions wrong, you are instructed to administer the first shock. It is disturbing when you hear him say "Ouch" through the intercom. The experiment progresses. He continues to get more answers wrong, and the severity of the shock continues to rise, as do his cries of pain. It is becoming obvious that your partner is suffering with each jolt of electricity. After you reach the 120 volts mark, the student in the experiment shouts into the intercom, "That's all! Get me out of here! Get me out of here, please! Let me out!"

As you turn to look at the researcher, expecting him to pull the plug, you are surprised when he simply replies, "It is imperative that the experiment continues." What do you do? Listen to the researcher, or tell him that you refuse to inflict pain on an innocent person who does not want to participate anymore.

If you're like the majority of the people who participated in this experiment, you continue to administer the shocks despite the pleas from the student. In fact, about two-thirds of the people in this study continued shocking their partner all the way up to the maximum 450 volts. Even more surprising is that not one of the 40 subjects refused to administer the shocks when the victim first demanded his release, or later when he begged to be let out. It was not until the experiment reached 300 volts that a few subjects finally "quit" and refused to comply any longer with the researcher's requests.

Before you become too horrified, you should know something. The student volunteer—the one who was getting shocked—was really an actor paid to play the part. But participants were not told this, so in their mind they really were shocking the student for every wrong answer. Milgram was looking to see how much pain an individual was willing to inflict on an innocent person when it was their job.

People were shocked and disturbed by the results of the study. And other studies have since been repeated with similar results. How could everyday normal people, who were psychologically healthy, behave in such ways? This experiment and others like it reveal the powerful social force of weighted relationships.

Whether it is a security guard asking you to put a dime in a parking meter or a researcher asking you to administer a shock or a boss asking you to stay an extra half-hour at work, an inexplicable force acts upon us when a person in authority requires us to do something. From the time we were young, we have been taught to listen to—and obey—

authority. It's not a bad thing. In fact, without submission to authority, our society would not function. And because it is so ingrained in our psychology, authority figures such as bosses, managers, coaches, and teachers have special leverage in our lives to influence us. If you don't believe me, then the next time you think your boss should be doing things differently go and tell him or her to change! Chances are you wouldn't have a problem telling your coworkers what to do, or maybe even making suggestions to your peers. But when it comes to giving advice upwards, we have to overcome incredibly large internal barriers just to have the boldness to get the words out of our mouth.

People who hold positions of authority in our lives leave their mark on us because we naturally open ourselves up to be influenced. This is why you can probably tell me the name of every boss you have ever worked for, every head coach you have ever played for, and every grade school teacher you have ever studied under, but you can't recall all the names of your coworkers, teammates, or classmates. Leaders become part of our life story, and they have the ability to leave either good memories and experiences or bad ones.

In the same way, the people you lead have naturally opened themselves up to your influence simply because of the title you hold. It has been ingrained in them since they were two years old. While some call this positional authority, the concept of weighted relationships goes far beyond that. It's not about pulling rank, but rather the potential leverage you gain because of the position itself. There have been many who have abused this power to the detriment of others, but leaders who have integrity recognize it not so much as an asset but rather as a giant responsibility.

Leaders who understand the principle of weighted relationships take the responsibility of leading others seriously and understand that they have the power to add to someone's quality of life, or take away from it. As a friend once said to me, "It's not really what job you're doing as much as it is who you are working for." Her comment is echoed by millions of others. A Saratoga Institute study found that a manager's behavior was the number one factor in determining an employee's happiness at work, and a Gallup Organization study, based on interviews over 25 years with 12 million workers, found that an employee's relationship with a manager largely determines an employee's length of stay with the organization. The old saying appears to be true, "People don't quit jobs; they quit managers."

This also means that the opposite is true. Many people love their job because they like working for their manager. As a manager you represent the company.

One time I was doing some coaching for a large energy company. I recall some managers speaking about the organization in glowing terms, while another manager told me how lousy the company was and how he predicted a mass exodus after bonuses were given out. I remember being astonished by the diversity of views regarding the same company. What was going on here? It turns out that the differences of view all came back to how the individual was being managed. We have all heard stories of people resigning from a great company because they couldn't stand their boss. On the flip side, we have also seen people stay with a dysfunctional organization because they enjoyed working for their manager.

When it comes to having weight as a manager, the following are areas where we need to pay close attention:

1. *Your way:* Everybody has a certain way of doing things. Whether you want to call it your brand or your culture, the point is that everyone has a certain style of leading shaped by beliefs, values, and past experiences. This, of course, spills over into your team and helps shape a mini subculture within your organization. It's a bit like being the mayor of a small town with each of your direct reports living within your jurisdiction. People care more about what's happening in their local community than at a regional or

state level. The question is, what is it like to live in your town? We are probably the least competent ones to answer that question because it is difficult for us to see our own way. That's why 360-degree feedback assessments can be a useful tool when administered correctly, because they give us a slice of what it's like to live under our watch.

2. *Your words:* Your words carry weight. In one study it was found that 57 percent of employees would rather receive praise from their direct supervisor, as opposed to 21 percent who would prefer to hear it from the top. It is interesting that your words as a manager mean more to your employees than the same words of praise coming from the CEO. Have you ever had your boss say something really nice and uplifting to you? Hopefully so. There is a good chance that when you got home that day after work, you shared it with your spouse or significant other. Isn't it amazing that the words we say to our direct reports can affect how they feel when they get home and even what they pass on to loved ones. At my seminars I often ask people to respond if they have ever gone home in a bad mood because of their boss. The majority of those in the room raise their hands. I don't know about you, but I never asked for that much responsibility when I first signed up to lead. However, over time I have realized that this is all part of the mantle of leadership.

3. *Your actions and attitudes:* Last but not least, your actions and the example you set carry a lot of weight with your people. If your employees notice a coworker slacking off, it will certainly make them angry, but if they were to see you slacking off, it would have a profoundly different effect. If someone on your team shows up to work in a bad mood, people don't give it much thought other than to ask, "What's their problem?" However, if the boss shows up to work in a grouchy mood, word will spread quickly among the entire team, putting everyone on red alert to be careful and stay out of the boss's way.

My first real experience leading a significant number of people came when I was in my early twenties. I was responsible for a group of about 50. My group was not doing so well. Morale was low, people were leaving, and the situation didn't appear to be turning around despite my efforts. I, of course, took the position of blaming the circumstances around us as the reason for our dilemma.

My boss at the time was a man named Bob, a wise and demanding leader. To get things turned around, Bob decided to hold daily team meetings, which I was expected to attend. On the first day, we all took our seats and, after teaching some principles about leadership, Bob turned to me and began publicly challenging my work ethic and passion. It was a hard talk, the kind where everyone in the room feels sorry for you; yet at the same time they were relieved because they were not the ones on the receiving end.

The next day, when it was time for our meeting, I decided to sit in a new chair, figuring my usual one was unlucky. I soon found out that it had nothing to do with my choice of seat. Halfway through the meeting, Bob singled me out again, challenging me to make something happen and get things going. Day three rolled around. I was starting to hate daily team meetings and really starting to dislike Bob. Once again, Bob gave me special attention.

The interesting thing at the time is that Bob never wanted to meet with my team and deliver the same message he had challenged me with. That's because Bob knew the power of weighted relationships. He knew that if he got me going, I'd get them going. If he could relight my passion, I would relight theirs. Where I wanted to blame someone or something, Bob taught me that my group was where they were either because I had led them there or because I had allowed them to go there. Either way, I had to take ownership. While this may seem like a hard pill to swallow, it's essential to understand as a manager. The sooner you are able to take ownership of your group, the quicker you can get proactive and find a solution.

When we see the weight of our impact on the lives of those we lead, it's hard not to feel both sobered and inspired. Sobered because of the great responsibility to lead with excellence in order to contribute to, rather than take away from, our employees' quality of life. Inspired because of the great opportunity we have to help our people reach new levels of excellence. This sacred trust must motivate us to fully engage ourselves in our roles as managers while aspiring to a higher standard of leadership excellence. The best leaders are those who set their minds on the practice of influencing people. In order to do that, you must master the nine needs of employees at work.

LEADERSHIP TRUTH 2

On the mountain, the guide is responsible for the lives of the climbers.

TRANSLATION

As a leader, you carry a great responsibility. You have the potential for incredible impact on the lives of those you lead. Strive to lead with excellence.

(3)

The Nine Needs

Leadership should be born out of the understanding of
the needs of those who would be affected by it.

—Marian Anderson

I was raised on a ranch in the foothills of the Rocky Mountains. While the scenery was beautiful—even to a six-year-old boy—it was rivaled after dark by a canopy of stars, shouting from an unpolluted night sky. The Big Dipper was always prominent, and I was taught how to use it to locate Polaris, the North Star. How many sailors in centuries past had used these beacons in the sky to help navigate their way on the open sea? As long as the sky was clear, the stars would show themselves. Faithful and unchanging, they provided a map that, night after night, could be counted on to lead sailors home.

There has been a lot of talk about the speed of change, the multigenerational workforce, and the challenge to lead and motivate others. And while change is a reality, it is good to know that there are certain principles of the human condition relating to performance excellence that, like Polaris, remain true and unchanging, regardless of race, religion, culture, or generation. These principles, which at their core are fundamental human needs, lie at the heart of all great achievement. The last few decades of research in the fields of psychology, sociology, neuroscience, and human behavior have begun to shed light on these principles of human excellence. Aided by an ever-growing body of research, a map is beginning to emerge that, like the stars in the sky, has actually existed for more than a millennium. Despite our ever-changing world, these principles are universal. They are wound into the very fabric of who we are as a species and are available to anyone who desires to help other human beings tap into their potential. These principles are in fact human needs. Some of them we were born with, and others we have acquired along the way. Through my own research, along with years of working to help other leaders inspire the best in their people, I have identified nine core needs which, when met, ignite engagement and excellence in individuals.

It is helpful to visualize these needs as switches. Each time you turn one on, it unlocks a portion of potential inside another human being. The more switches you flip, the greater the potential for elevated performance. Show me a workplace that lacks motivation or suffers from poor morale, and I will show you a group of people who have very few—if any—of these nine switches turned on. On the other hand, whenever you hear of an organization filled with incredibly motivated employees, devoted and engaged in their jobs, you will find leaders who are helping meet many of the nine needs we discuss below.

Unlike actual switches, however, these needs cannot be met once and then forgotten. Just as our need for food and water must be continually satisfied, so too must these nine needs be nurtured on an ongoing basis.

Because not all needs are equal, I have divided them into two groups; the first four carry the most weight, and the remaining five round out the palette of workplace excellence. (See Figure 1.)

THE BIG FOUR

The primary four needs are:

1. *Care—the need to be more than a number:* Your ability to lead and influence is directly related to how much trust your employees have

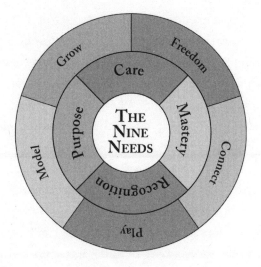

Figure 1

in you. Trust has several sources, but probably the most neglected is care. People want to know they are more than a number or a resource to be used. When employees feel that their organization cares about them as individuals, then they are willing to invest more of themselves in the job. As a manager, you must show your direct reports that they are indeed more than a number. When they feel you care, then they feel the organization cares. In Chapter 5 you will learn two practical ways to do this.

2. *Mastery—the need for challenge and achievement:* One of our deepest psychological needs is our need for mastery. We desire to engage in a challenge, struggle with it, and overcome. When you can provide moments of mastery for employees, you will see a dramatic spike in their effort, persistence, and intrinsic motivation. In Chapter 6 you will learn the three ingredients that can turn an employee's job into a source of mastery, and how you can take even the most mundane jobs and use them to meet the need for challenge and achievement.

3. *Recognition—the need to be appreciated:* From the time we were children, we have been socially conditioned to believe that what we produce is linked to our perception of how others value us. Because of this, people need to be appreciated and valued for the work they do and the effort they expend. When you as a manager master how to recognize employees in a way that increases their perception of value, you will ignite the fires of loyalty and increased effort. In Chapter 7 I show you how to move beyond generic statements like, "Great job," and develop what I call the Midas touch.

4. *Purpose—the need to contribute and be significant:* Deep down inside we all want our lives to count. Especially as we get older, we begin to pay more attention to the impact of our lives and the contribution we are making. Purpose is one of the most powerful motivators, and when you as a manager tap into it, members of your staff will engage emotionally with their work. In Chapter 8 I will show you three simple ways to link purpose to pay.

SECONDARY NEEDS

The following secondary needs are no less important than the big four, but they are better focused on once the primary needs are in place:

1. *Autonomy—the need to be in control:* For the majority of the world, freedom is prized. It turns out that freedom also encourages higher levels of motivation and self-initiation. When your employees feel a sense of autonomy, they will work harder, persist longer in the face of obstacles, think more flexibly and creatively when solving problems, and enjoy their work more. In Chapter 9 I will show you how to create more autonomy for your employees, which promotes personal buy-in and accountability.

2. *Growth—the need to progress:* Employees put a premium on growth because they know that in today's competitive labor market they must continually improve. Investing in your employees is one of

the most powerful drivers of employee engagement. The challenge is always time and money. In Chapter 10 I show you a simple and effective model which will help your direct reports grow without costing you hours of your time or money.

3. *Connection—the need to connect with others:* We have always been a social species; therefore, understanding the social dynamics of groups is essential for a great manager. A good team can increase productivity and morale, while a dysfunctional one can wipe out an entire staff. In Chapter 11 I show you how to create sticky teams, keep an eye on team morale, and which three dangers you must guard against to protect your team from morale erosion.

4. *Play—the need to enjoy work:* All work and no play makes Jack a dull boy. It also makes him more stressed, less creative, and reduces the amount of effort he puts into his job. Your employees spend a large part of their waking life at work and want to enjoy the journey. Whether you work at a funeral home or a circus, fun and laughter are important tools for inspiring higher levels of engagement and trust. In Chapter 12 I give you some practical ways to increase the fun quotient at your workplace without having to become a comedian or enroll in clown school.

5. *Model—the need for a path to follow:* The research is clear. In the eyes of your direct reports, no one's example is more important than yours. Modeling the way serves many purposes—inspiring trust and loyalty, providing security and confidence, and painting a picture to show how employees should act and even feel. Most managers know that they need to set an example, but few know what example they should be setting and when. The top leaders in the world not only set an example, but they know what to model and when. Different times require different examples to be set. In Chapter 13 I show you what your employees most need from you and how to purposely adjust your example so that it always matches the current landscape.

PRACTICE MAKES A LEADER

The key to motivating your employees and inspiring them to perform at their highest levels lies in your ability to administer these nine needs. Someone once said, "Knowledge is power"; however, when it comes to engaging your staff, simply knowing the nine needs is not enough. They must be applied practically. I believe that anyone can grow in their ability to do this. Too many managers don't practice leadership. It's as if we expect leadership to come naturally or that common sense should carry us through, but the reality is that motivating others is a skill, and skills can be learned. Whether you are just starting out on your leadership journey or have been leading people for decades, your leadership can become more effective by deliberate practice. This book will show you how by laying out the practical steps you can take.

LEADERSHIP TRUTH 3

No one is born a mountain guide. Guiding comes with practice.

TRANSLATION

Leadership is a practice.
The more you work at it, the better a leader you will become.

(4)

Airplanes Need Pilots, Not Janitors

*The absent are never without fault, nor the present
without excuse.*

—Benjamin Franklin

If you were flying into Miami on Eastern Airlines flight 401 the night of December 29, 1972, nothing would have alerted you that a problem was brewing. Members of the flight crew were making their last rounds, ensuring that seat backs were forward, carry-on luggage was safely stowed beneath the seats, and tray tables were upright and in their locked position. With the lights of Miami dancing below you, there was nothing unusual about this scene—no cause for concern. But as the ground grew closer, your descent was suddenly interrupted by the plane's three engines as they roared to life, pushing you back into your seat, and the plane began climbing sharply into the night sky. While you and your fellow passengers looked around at each other quizzically, a story was unfolding in the cockpit.

The captain, copilot, and flight engineer were following standard procedure as they prepared to bring the Tristar L 1011 safely to the tarmac. After checking the braking system, radar, and hydraulics, it was time to lower the landing gear.

Below the lever that lowers the wheels there are three lights, corresponding to the three sets of landing gear on the plane. When they activated the switch to lower the landing gear, there was a problem. Two lights illuminated as they should have, but the middle light representing the front wheels remained dark.

Either the front wheels had not descended or the light bulb that confirmed that the wheels were down had burned out. Not wanting to take any chances, the captain aborted the landing by climbing to the safety of 2,000 feet. From there they could begin a straightforward procedure known as Problem Solving 101.

While the navigation officer left the cockpit to attempt a visual from below deck, the captain and copilot attempted to change the light bulb. The tiny bulb, however, would not release. For the next seven minutes, both the captain and copilot focused their attention on the tiny light. After it was finally removed, the light became jammed when they tried to push it back in. It was during this time that something critical happened. The plane began to descend.

It appears that the autopilot may have been disengaged by accident when one of the crew members bumped against it. The resulting altitude loss would have been apparent on their instrument panels, but unfortunately those were not being monitored. The challenge of fixing the tiny light bulb now consumed all of the pilots' attention and, with the autopilot disengaged, no one was flying the plane.

The passengers must have assumed that the descent was part of their final approach to land and probably sat patiently, waiting to feel the bump of tires on the runway. The flight attendants were doing what flight attendants do; preparing the cabin and passengers for their arrival in Miami. The only ones not doing what they usually do were the pilots. Pilots fly planes; yet, even with over 50,000 hours of flying experience among the three of them, no one was flying flight 401.

As the plane reached 500 feet, an altitude alarm sounded in the cockpit, but no one appears to have heard it. While continuing to work on the tiny light bulb, the pilots were oblivious to the fact that they were about to slam into the everglades. The control tower at Miami airport radioed flight 401 to find out what was happening.

Here is the recorded conversation during the last 30 seconds of Eastern Airlines Flight 401:

Tower: Eastern, ah, 401, how are things coming along out there?
Cockpit: Okay, we'd like to turn around and come, come back in.
Pilot: Clear on left?
Copilot: Okay.
Tower: Eastern 401 turn left heading one eight zero.
Pilot: Huh?
Cockpit: One eighty.
Copilot: We did something to the altitude.
Pilot: What?
Copilot: We're still at two thousand, right?
Pilot: Hey, what's happening here?
Cockpit [Sound of click]
Cockpit [Sound of six beeps similar to radio altimeter increasing in rate]
[Sound of impact]

By the time the copilot realized they were not at an altitude of 2,000 feet but, rather, at less than 100 feet, it was too late to correct. The aircraft slammed into the ground, killing 103 passengers onboard. How do three pilots with over 50,000 hours of flying time among them crash an airplane? They failed to look at their instrument panel. Were they bad pilots? Before you answer, consider this. Every year in the United States 15 to 20 children die because someone leaves them in a vehicle on a hot day. How does a loving, devoted parent become distracted and forget that his or her child is in the car? Are they all bad mothers and fathers? I don't believe so. And I don't believe that the crew of flight 401 were bad pilots, but they *were* fatally distracted at the most crucial time, and when people in positions of authority are led away from their highest priorities, the consequences can be severe.

MY HAIR IS ON FIRE

What happened that night on flight 401 is an accurate metaphor for the biggest challenge managers face: neglecting our priorities as leaders while losing ourselves in the daily changing of lightbulbs. Our workplaces are more complex, stressful, and demanding than ever, and yet our brains have a limit to how many things they can devote their attention to at any given time. While flight 401 is an extreme case of the price of distracted leadership, a similar, albeit less tragic form plagues workplaces around the world.

We have been told by management gurus and leadership experts alike that our most important asset is our people. It sounds right, and it even looks good on our mission statements hanging in the lobby of our corporate headquarters, but in today's hectic environment the ideal of "people first" often gives way to the pressures of next week's deadlines.

I have spoken to many managers who confess that they are just too busy to lead their people effectively. In fact, one manager said to me, "It's hard to be strategic when your hair is on fire." I often pass this quote on when speaking to managers, who laugh and nod their heads, identifying with the struggle. It would have been much easier for Osvaldo to leave us at 20,000 feet and continue on to the summit himself, but he was not being paid to climb mountains, but rather to help us climb one.

Some managers are so busy that leaving their desk in order to manage their staff likely means that they themselves will not be able to get all their work done by the end of the day. And while striving hard to shorten our list of tasks, meet our deadlines, and juggle all the plates on our desk, it's quite easy to forget to look up and check our instrument panel to make sure that everyone is still flying at 2,000 feet. While we work hard trying to replace tiny lightbulbs, we have to make sure that a similar kind of fatal distraction is not taking place onboard our aircraft. While probably not costing physical lives, the toll can still be heavy, manifesting itself in low morale, costly employee turnover, and millions of dollars a year in lost productivity. Although the cost of distracted leadership can be high, I believe that much of it is not the result of managers who don't care or who don't know how to lead, but rather of leaders who are simply struggling to spin 11 different plates on 10 fingers.

THE QUINTESSENTIAL SKILL OF LEADERSHIP

Wally Berg is an American climber with an impressive résumé. He has stood at the top of Mt. Everest four times and has had six successful ascents on 8,000-meter peaks, including Cho Oyu, and Lhotse, at which he was the first American to reach the summit. Under his leadership, hundreds of people have reached the tops of the Seven Summits, the continental high points around the globe. Despite ascending to lofty heights, Wally remains down to earth and a genuinely humble and caring man. It was Wally's company, Berg Adventures, which would eventually take me to Bolivia.

One day I had the opportunity to interview Wally on leadership, a favorite topic of mine.

"Wally," I said, "you have led a lot of expeditions in your life, but you have also assisted on many other expeditions. In all of your years of climbing, who has stood out to you as an amazing leader?"

Without any hesitation Wally answered, "In all my years on Everest, one man, one climber who strikes me as a great leader is a fellow by the name of Apa Sherpa, who holds the record for most summits on Mt. Everest."

Wally went on to say many complimentary things about Apa, highlighting his focus and commitment, but at least six times during the interview Wally mentioned the same trait about Apa Sherpa that I call the quintessential skill of leadership. I say *quintessential* because I believe it is the quality that separates the good from the best. In fact, if you grow in this skill, your leadership will skyrocket in effectiveness. It is the very thing that would have saved flight 401 that fateful night in December.

The quintessential skill of leadership is *awareness*.

Wally told me that Apa Sherpa was aware—always paying attention to what was going on around him. Awareness is the art of being mindful of the circumstances around us while not losing sight of our highest priorities. Much is said about the power of focus, and it is true that great leaders are focused. But when a focus becomes too narrow, it blinds us to our surroundings. As a manager, our surroundings are critical. Awareness can be very difficult, especially with the mountain of things that cry out for our time on a daily basis. Awareness is all about balancing our attention. On one hand, if we lack focus, it is easy for our days to fill up with a lot of activity but little progress. On the other hand, if we let our focus narrow too much on any certain task (like changing a lightbulb), we can lose touch with important cues around us that might be critical in our journey.

Imagine for a moment Apa Sherpa guiding a group of clients up Mt. Everest. He is focused on the task at hand, yet always in tune with the environment—looking for signs of danger, monitoring weather, and assessing clients' energy levels. Apa Sherpa is a leader.

Leading people is a bit like climbing Mt. Everest. It is a complicated endeavor made even more difficult by ever-changing conditions. It requires the perfect balance of presence of mind and focus. For many managers today the competing demands for our attention cause us to become lost in a sea of to-do's, which can steal us away from our highest priorities: helping our people to be what we need them to be.

Let's return to the cockpit of flight 401 for a moment. While the pilots fiddled with the tiny lightbulb, imagine that they had a system to protect them from becoming too distracted. Some might argue that they already had everything they needed: altimeters, flight speed gauges, and so on. But what if they had a system in place that didn't allow them to become distracted? Something that would have forced them to look up and take notice, the way a mother turns a young child's head with her hand so he sees the approaching car before attempting to cross the street. A system like that would have saved 103 people on the night of December 29, 1972, by drawing the pilot's attention to what mattered most—flying the plane.

And what if, as a manager, you had a similar safeguard that would lift your head up, enabling you to quickly read your instrument panel and make the correct adjustments before returning to some of the managerial tasks that are required of you? What if you had a simple tool that made you aware of what is going on with your team, with morale, with motivation, and with your alignment? What if you were consistently addressing the nine needs of employee engagement in a way that was not onerous or burdensome to you?

That is what *Nine Minutes on Monday* is all about; a simple system to keep you aware of the key drivers that inspire and bring out the best in your people. The key to any system, however, is that it must be sustainable. Too many programs look exciting enough initially, but because of their complexity, they fail to produce long-term results. The best solutions are simple, yet effective, in keeping you focused on your most important priorities. Of course, this does require some type of change in how we do things, and change is hard. *Nine Minutes on Monday* is designed to help you make simple changes to your weekly schedule that will enhance your leadership effectiveness. When it comes to motivating your staff members and bringing out their best, there is no magic bullet, because great leadership is more about the small things done consistently than some huge one-time initiative. In order to see long-term results, however, you must be willing to stay the course. The problem with making long-term changes is that we are fighting against established routines and habits. In order to succeed we must overcome two barriers in the change process.

WHY MOST CHANGE FAILS

My wife is a nutritionist, personal trainer, and weight loss expert. She helps people get into shape and lose weight. One would think that I would be in better shape than I am. Whenever she meets with a prospective client, she can tell within the first five minutes whether or not the person will be successful in losing weight. The key? Those who make excuses and blame their weight gain on life circumstances don't stand a chance. But the ones who, regardless of why they put on the weight, accept personal responsibility are the ones who stand a chance. Until you own it, you will never change it. The same principle can be applied to management. Those who are filled with excuses as to why they cannot engage their staff, never will. I once met with a business owner who wished me luck when I was about to meet with his people. He had stopped believing that they were capable of being motivated. After spending an hour with them, I saw that they really *did* want to excel in their jobs, contrary to what their boss had told me. The good news about the members of your staff is that they can be motivated and engaged to produce at high levels of excellence. The other piece of good news is that you are a large part of the formula in creating a highly motivated workplace that is within your control. Own your responsibility, and you will be ready to make long-lasting changes.

The second reason why change often fails is that people try to change too much at once. Life demands enough from all of us so that we usually arrive at the end of our day with the tank empty. Any change that diverts us from our usual routine taxes our resources both mentally and physically. A classic example is again from the world of weight loss. It is January 1 and my wife's phone starts ringing—calls from people determined to turn over a new leaf. They urgently want to meet with her and are determined to get started on a complete life overhaul. They show up with promises that they will eat healthier and exercise regularly and want to know what steps to take. The problem with weight loss is much like the problems involved in transforming our leadership. We are working against old ways. Many people committed to losing weight attempt to do a complete 180-degree turn by ridding their house of junk food, overhauling their diet, and showing up at the gym four times a week. While all of these are the right things to do, by trying to do too much at once, they are usually on the path to failure. What started out as great intention soon morphs into excuses and a relapse into old ways. The plan was correct and the desire was there, so what happened? They simply ran out of steam. Something similar is seen in management when we attend a seminar on leadership and return to the office with 5 pages of notes and 30 new things we want to implement. While all 30 things may help your leadership, the chances of you making the changes stick are slim to none.

If people want to lose weight, they will do better if they can see it as a lifestyle change and one that is made gradually. My wife may tell a client to simply start by swapping their breakfast for a healthier option and work out for 10 minutes a couple of times a week. While this may seem frustratingly slow for clients, it helps them make progress at a slower pace which, in the end, will be more self-sustaining. A week later, once they have mastered a different approach to breakfast, she might tell them to start replacing lunch with healthier options and to increase their workout times to 15 minutes.

Nine Minutes on Monday is designed to help you transform your leadership slowly, implementing small steps. Each step may seem insignificant on its own but, when added together, they form a journey leading ever closer to the summit.

FIXED LINES

We were around 16,500 feet with only 1,000 feet left to the summit of Pequenyo Alpamayo, a gem of a peak in Bolivia. The path to the summit from here lay along a jagged knife-edge ridge with a serious fall on either side. It was not the kind of place where you could afford to make a mistake and, possessing a serious fear of heights, I was definitely having second thoughts. Reaching the summit hinged on making sure you stayed on track without veering too far to the left or right, both of which would have tragic consequences. It is times like these, if you're not an experienced climber, that you hire professional guides to get you to where you are going.

As I waited at the bottom, Osvaldo skillfully made his way up the ridge, his crampons biting into the snow with each step. I remember feeling nervous for him knowing that a fall on this steep section could be fatal. However, Osvaldo, being a professional, skillfully navigated the terrain and began attaching a safety line to the mountain. This is called a fixed line. Fixed lines are part of an important safety system often used in dangerous sections while climbing. The guides ascend ahead of you and attach long ropes to the mountain with long ice pickets. Then, with a small hand-held tool called an ascender, you simply clip onto the line and follow it until you reach your destination.

A fixed line is a brilliant, yet simple, concept to protect you if you make a mistake, and ensures that you stay on track. It also frees up mental energy that is needed to stay in tune with the environment.

Nine Minutes on Monday is like your fixed line, leading you up the mountain of leadership excellence. Clip in and follow, and each week, with each small step, you will get closer to the top. *Nine Minutes* is a simple system to keep you from being buried in an avalanche of tasks, all the while keeping the most important principles of leadership in front of you. By keeping your awareness on your most important asset—your people—you make the dramatic shift from manager to inspirational leader.

THE MOST IMPORTANT NINE MINUTES OF YOUR WEEK

For years I have been teaching managers to develop what I call a leadership planning time. It simply involves taking some time every Monday morning to think through your leadership priorities for the week ahead. As a manager you may already do a good job in planning your tasks for the week. Every Monday morning you might look at your calendar, review your deadlines, or create a to-do list for the week. Leadership planning time is different. It is specifically devoted to helping you think through your leadership priorities and what you will need to do this week to help move your people. Just as Osvaldo sat for a few minutes at 20,000 feet thinking about what he should do next in order to move us farther up the mountain, the leadership planning time is devoted to this same type of thinking. In fact, these few moments where you think through your leadership for the week are arguably the most important minutes in your entire week, because it is here that you will lift your head up, glance at your instrument panel, and make decisions that are going to have an effect on your staff's performance.

The key to long-term success is to hold to this time religiously until it becomes carved into your weekly routine. You want the leadership planning time to become ritual. The beautiful thing about it is that it does not require a lot of your time. Only minutes—nine of them to be exact. The secret, however, is not simply holding to the ritual itself, but rather what you think through during your leadership planning time that makes the difference. As we move on to Part II of this book, we will unpack the nine needs in greater detail, and I will show you how to condense each of them into a simple question to ask yourself each and every Monday as you get ready to begin your week.

LISTO?

When we were climbing in South America, our guides would often say to us, "Listo?" as we were gearing up. This means, "Ready?" in Spanish. And we would reply, "Listo!" and then clip onto the rope. Over the coming pages I want you to "clip in" and follow along as we ascend this mountain together. I guarantee that you are going to learn some new tools that will help you bring out the best in those you lead.

Listo?

KEY LESSONS

- The biggest enemy of leadership is overcommitment to tasks.
- Keeping your leadership priorities in front of you is essential to effective management.
- Spend nine minutes every Monday morning to plan your leadership for the week ahead.

PART II

Primary Needs

Grandpa Jack and Big Al
The Need to Be More Than a Number

A kind word is like a spring day.
—Russian proverb

I remember when my wife and I were first married and needed to buy a car. To save some money, we ventured over to the industrial part of town where there were several discount car lots, like the one with the big sign that reads something like, "Big Al's Cars," with long strings of tiny triangular flags fluttering in the wind. The cars are jammed onto a gravel lot with prices written on the windshields, and a small trailer with caged windows sits off to one side. As you drive up, a man dressed in a suit from two decades ago emerges from the trailer. This must be Big Al, you assume. With an ear-to-ear grin and a swagger in his step, Big Al approaches, and as he does, you feel a tightening in your stomach. You arm your defenses, preparing for the pitch.

This inner resistance is part of our natural defense mechanism telling us to be on guard in potentially threatening situations. The danger here, of course, is that Big Al just might try to take advantage of you. It's during times like these that we "play our cards close to our vest" or put on our "poker face"; just a couple of the many available countermeasures we can use in this type of situation. This strategy of defense is meant to limit the amount of influence that others can exert on our lives. Your defensive posture poses a challenge for Big Al, whose success largely depends on his ability to influence you, all of which hinges on something we call trust.

So the game begins as the car salesman initiates various trust-building techniques—a friendly smile, asking about your golf game—from information he gathered by spotting your clubs in the back seat of your car as you drove up. The battle is not so much for your money as it is for your trust.

Big Al might actually be a nice guy. In fact, he may be genuinely sincere, but the fact remains that most people initially will not trust him. Justified or not, the majority of us assume that Big Al wants something from us—our money. When we suspect that people are trying to take us for a ride, we proceed with caution and simply resist their influence. At the end of the day, trust is influence. Without it, your leadership will be severely hindered.

YOUR TRUST ACCOUNT

Because leadership hinges on your ability to influence people, you want to do everything you can to build trust among your employees. Regardless of what industry you are in, if you are a manager, the currency you deal in is trust. Imagine trust as a bank account. The goal is to keep your balance perpetually high. When your account runs dangerously low, you bankrupt your ability to influence and motivate. When your trust account is full, your leadership balloons in terms of effectiveness. Without trust there is no influence, and without influence there will be limited results. As a manager, trust is your best friend. It provides you with leverage when you have to move people to action. Without it you may be able to hire your employees' hands, but you will never employ their hearts, and without heart, their performance will always fall short of their potential.

THE TRINITY OF TRUST

A recent survey found that the more trust an employee has in his or her manager, the higher their engagement.

There are several reasons for this, but one that is often overlooked is that a high trust environment is safe. Safety is something we all value. If you head over to Big Al's cars, and Big Al just happens to be your father, your experience will be entirely different from that of a potential customer. When we feel safe, we don't have to waste valuable energy scanning the environment for signs of danger. Safety allows us to focus and apply ourselves without holding back. The more we trust, the safer we feel. But where does trust originate, and how do we make deposits to our trust account? There are three primary sources from which the rivers of trust flow. I call these three the *trinity of trust,* and each one is essential in understanding how it is built. The three sources are: character, competence, and caring.

Character

Character is the single most important factor in building trust. Like it or not, there is a strong moral expectation of anyone in leadership. Yet, according to a poll by Maritz Research, only 11 percent of employees strongly agree that their managers show consistency between their words and actions. Character is what your employees see when they look at you. It is your example, your values, your work ethic, your integrity, and your perceived honesty. As a leader, your example is magnified because of the weighted relationship we discussed earlier.

I remember at one of our end-of-year Christmas banquets, I went around after dinner clearing off some of the tables. One of our volunteers told me later how much that had affected him. While I had no idea that something so simple would make a difference, it demonstrates how closely people watch your example when you are in a position of leadership. In one classic study done by Kouzes and Posner, it was found that the number-one attribute employees wanted in their managers was honesty. The reason for these findings, of course, is honesty's direct link to integrity and trust. Employees want to work in an environment where they can trust their bosses. When managers lead with integrity and consistency of example, it creates a bedrock foundation that employees can rely on. The key ingredient in trust building as it relates to character is time. Trust built on character is powerful, but it is not accomplished overnight. Like sedimentary rock, it is built layer by layer, as deposits are made consistently over time.

Competence

Not all the sources of trust take an extended time. It was 2:30 a.m., under the cover of darkness, that I met Osvaldo, our mountain guide, for the first time. My life was placed in his hands within two hours of our first handshake. This did not allow me much time to build trust in him. On this particular day we were attempting to climb a beautiful mountain named Pequeño Alpamayo. It is a very popular peak among climbers as it rises out of the Andes like a pristine pyramid set against the most magnificent deep blue sky.

The final path to the summit lay along a knife-edged ridge that fell away for hundreds of feet on either side. Because I have a fear of heights, I was not looking forward to it. For safety, I was told I would be short-roped to a more experienced guide who had arrived late the night before. Short-roping is exactly as it sounds—you and a more experienced climber are connected by a short length of rope. The idea is that if you fall, the guide will be able to stop you from sliding down the mountain into one of the yawning crevasses and an icy grave.

I knew nothing of Osvaldo's character, but I had heard that he was an experienced guide and climber. His competence in climbing helped me extend the necessary trust to make our attempt a success. Competence, like character, is a source of trust. When employees feel that you are capable of leading effectively, they are willing to place more trust in you as a manager. As a manager, competence does not equate to knowing more than everyone else on your team. Such a position of superiority will actually backfire. This is a lesson I learned as a young leader, mistakenly believing that I must have all the answers. Competence as a manager has more to do with your ability to manage and lead people effectively. This is not so much a matter of technical skills as it is an issue of understanding people. The safest way forward is to remain genuinely humble and committed to growth in your own personal leadership. As I mentioned earlier, practice makes a leader.

Caring

One of the most neglected ingredients of the trust trinity, and the focus of the rest of this chapter, is the ability to show that you care. Let's wander off Big Al's car lot for a moment and down the street to Grandpa Jack's house. Grandpa Jack is old and wise. He likes to sit in a rocking chair on the front porch with his golden retriever lying faithfully by his side. We trust Grandpa Jack—perhaps not to carry the baby down the stairs—but we trust Grandpa Jack with almost everything else. Why is that? One of the most obvious reasons is that Grandpa Jack cares. He does not want anything *from* you. In fact, he just wants what's best *for* you. While your parents may be pressuring you to get a college degree, Grandpa Jack is usually the one who encourages you to pursue your dreams. In short, he cares for you apart from what you do for him.

We like to know that we are cared about, and we hate being used. But what does this have to do with employee excellence? Does caring for your employees have a place in management advice? A recent worldwide survey of over 90,000 employees says it does. In fact, the study revealed that the number-one driver of employee engagement was, "When senior management takes a genuine interest in me as an individual." Employees do not want to be just a number or another cog in the wheel. They actually want to feel cared about by their bosses. According to a Maritz Research poll, only 7 percent of employees strongly agree they trust senior leaders to look out for their best interest.

When people show us they care, we can't help but reciprocate by doling out a little trust. It's as if we place a small deposit in their trust account. This is a huge deal because essentially we are saying, "I'm opening myself up to be influenced by you."

So, on one end of the street we have Big Al who only wants something *from* you, and on the other end we have Grandpa Jack who simply wants the best *for* you. As a manager, we can't adhere to either end of the spectrum, but we had better lean more toward Grandpa Jack's end of the street than that of the shady car salesman. Still, too many managers treat their employees like numbers, or simple resources, attempting to squeeze as much out of them as they can. If your employees feel that you care, then they will trust you, and if they trust you, then you have opened the door of influence.

To be cared about is one of our basic needs as humans. We want to know that we count, that we matter, and that people really do have our backs. Because we spend so much time at work, we naturally look for some of these needs to be met there. As a manager, it can be easy to get into the car salesperson's mode, constantly needing and wanting things from our employees. "What have you done for me today?"

While I understand that people are paid to produce, we are talking here about maximizing engagement. People *do* want to work, and they *do* want to give you what you need, but they also want to know that you care. If they sense that they are simply a resource to be used, they will never fully engage and may soon be looking for a new employer who promises them more.

When you begin to talk about caring workplaces, some people become downright squeamish. From the outside this can look like nothing more than soft fluffy stuff, which may have been great in grade school, but this is the real world. After all, we can't go around hugging everyone in the workplace. Fortunately, creating a more caring workplace has nothing to do with hugging and is a lot easier than you think.

SHOWING YOU CARE

Paul was an efficient manager with great self-awareness. As a child he had been raised in a Communist bloc country and recognized that sometimes his natural style of managing might come across as a bit blunt and harsh for the North American work culture. When I began coaching Paul, he wanted to improve his soft skills. He was a typical manager—hardworking, overloaded, and spending too much time in meetings. His discretionary time was almost nonexistent. Even our coaching sessions stretched his schedule. I began by teaching Paul the power of being interested. What you are interested in is where your attention will be. Because of this, it is only natural that managers show an interest in what their people are producing. "Mary, where is the report?" "Sam, how is the proposal coming?" "Parker, get me Spiderman!" If you want your employees to feel that you genuinely care about them as people and that they are more than a number within your organization, the simplest way to begin is by taking an interest in their lives. The easiest place to start is with what I call their vital statistics.

Vital Statistics

Most governments have some form of vital statistics that they keep for all their citizens. These include such information as birth certificates, marriage licenses, and death certificates. This information is of great interest to governments for obvious reasons. In the same way, every person has a circle of interests they would consider "vital" to their life, such as family, close friends, and perhaps a hobby or two. Along with their work, this pretty much makes up what is "vital" to most human beings. Taking even a little bit of time to show a genuine interest in someone's vital statistics communicates that you care.

As a manager, as long as you don't have too many direct reports (more than 10), here are some things you should know about each of your employees:

- Their spouse's or partner's name
- Their children's names
- A major hobby of theirs

If you really want to strive for world-class status, then also know the health condition of their aging parents.

There are many reasons why you want to know an employee's vital statistics, but the primary one is that it provides a jumping-off point for you to begin showing ongoing genuine interest in their lives. In addition to feeling cared about, your direct reports will feel that you value them for more than just what they bring to the job. These little things extend a long way, but unfortunately are not common among leaders. If they were, then the facts that Nelson Mandela used to know how his security guards took their coffee, or that Alexander the Great called his soldiers by their first names, would not have been mentioned in books written about them.

When Whitney's boss asks her how her daughter's ballet recital went over the weekend, the question alone communicates to her that she means more to the company than what she produces. It subtly adds to the message that she is a real person. This encourages her to trust and put more of her heart into her work.

Collecting Vital Statistics

For some managers, all this is so natural that they would be shocked after reading the last few pages.

"Doesn't everyone already do this?" they might ask. The truth is that many managers don't. Most of the time it's not that they don't care. It's simply a matter of letting their schedule crowd out these little things that produce big results. If you are a manager and you realize that you know hardly any of your employees' vital statistics, then here are a few tips.

Begin learning about your direct reports, but do it slowly and naturally. Give yourself a few months to fill in the picture. If you suddenly try gathering all of this information at once, your staff might wonder what you are up to. Instead of building trust, you might end up creating paranoia. This, of course, is not information you want to collect via survey. Imagine Sally filling out a form asking her whether her parents are alive or not! Take it slow and make it genuine. Showing you care is not a management technique but rather something you do because you are a leader. The additional benefit of knowing more about your employees is that it helps improve your ability to communicate. When you have even the slightest idea of some of the issues your staff may be going through, it dramatically changes how you communicate and how you approach motivating them.

The Walkabout

After explaining the concept of vital statistics to Paul, I asked him to start going on a weekly walkabout. The walkabout, I explained, was a time you set in your schedule that allows you to get out among your employees, simply to show interest in them. It is not a time to ask Kelly where the report is, but rather to ask her how her daughter Chelsea's soccer tournament went on the weekend. When I first asked Paul to do a walkabout, he complained that he did not have time. He was already in too many meetings and that his schedule was crazy. I explained that the walkabout did not have to take long. Even 10 minutes would begin to make an impact, to which Paul replied, "Ten minutes! But I have ten direct reports. That's 100 minutes!"

When I clarified that I meant only 10 minutes in total and that he didn't have to talk to each and every employee, he agreed to give it a try.

I followed up with Paul a bit later.

"Paul, how did your walkabout go?" I asked.

"Fantastic," he said. "I spent one hour talking with some of my directs."

While Paul didn't need to spend an entire hour, the exercise opened his eyes to how valuable this concept was. Despite his busy schedule, Paul decided to carve out time every Wednesday to conduct a walkabout. He later told me that this simple exercise had transformed his leadership. It isn't any wonder that, months later, when one of his talented direct reports was offered a position in another company for more money, she declined. When I asked her why, she told me she likes working for Paul.

What Will They Say About You in 20 Years?

In case you are still in doubt about the power of taking an interest in your employees, consider the following story. I was teaching a group of leaders about the concept of the walkabout when a young woman in the group put up her hand. She told the rest of us how her father used to manage a hotel and that he made it a point to know at least one thing about every one of his staff members. He would routinely walk around asking his employees simple questions, such as, "Hey Joe, how is Nancy doing?" She went on to explain that she often travels back home to visit her father and, while walking through the shopping mall, people will routinely recognize him and come up to say hello. She said these former employees often turn to her and say something like, "I worked for your father 20 years ago, and he used to always ask me how my wife was doing, or how my kids were doing."

Years later, what people remembered about this hotel manager was that he took an interest in them as people. One company I consulted for had a CEO who used to come down weekly from the ivory towers of the executive suite to mingle among the employees. He simply made the rounds engaging in small talk and showing a genuine interest in the company's employees. He has since stopped this practice and one of the managers confided to me, "Yeah, I really miss that."

When you show the members of your staff that they are more than a number, they will place more trust in you. And, as you already know, the more they trust you, the more influence you will have.

Taking an interest in your employees' vital statistics does more than just communicate that you care; it has the added benefit of improving communication. The better you know your employees, the better you are able to communicate. For example, when you know that Sally's mother is terminally ill, a fact that will add a ton of stress and emotion to her life, it will change the way you communicate. You may approach her differently on an issue or you may cut her some slack when she uncharacteristically snaps at someone. Because you are aware of what is going on, you are able to make adjustments in how you communicate and how you motivate.

Lift a Load

While no one expects you to be a counselor or therapist at work, there is incredible power in empathy. One of my favorite quotes is from Plato: "Be kind, for everyone you meet is carrying a heavy load." Each of your direct reports will go through times of carrying heavy burdens. Maybe they're struggling to care for aging parents, or one of their children has just received a challenging diagnosis, or they are in the midst of a messy relationship breakup. Simply inquiring about how they are doing through such times can do a lot to communicate that you care. No one is asking or expecting you to solve anything, but a simple inquiry or statement of encouragement to someone in the midst of a trial will demonstrate that they are more to you than merely a number.

A few years ago, a friend of mine went through a significant marital crisis. His wife dropped the news that she was leaving him for one of her coworkers. Because he could not pay the rent on his own, he was forced to move out of his house the following weekend. He explained to his boss what had happened and, since he was new to the city, asked her if she knew where he could find a moving truck. She asked him to leave it with her and returned 30 minutes later. She had found him a truck and had also arranged for a couple of the team members to come and help him move on Friday during work hours. Then she gave him the name and number of someone within the organization who could help him understand some of the employee benefits that might be available to him in his situation. How do you think my friend felt about his boss and his workplace after that?

Take an Interest in Their Future

Few things are closer to our hearts than our own personal ambitions, goals, and dreams. They are very personal, and we do not share them with just anyone. When someone not only takes an interest in where our lives are heading, but also wants to help us get there, we feel an incredible bond of goodwill and trust. Being interested in your employees' future plans and career goals can go a long way toward showing them they are more than a number.

Boardwalk and Park Place

A lot of organizations have their own unique rituals when it comes to celebrating birthdays, and some are better than others. Birthdays are like "Boardwalk" in the game of Monopoly—important pieces of real estate that you don't want to miss. Unfortunately, some companies try too hard when it comes to celebrating birthdays, turning them into a rotating burden throughout the year. Someone is charged with getting the cake; someone else has to get everyone to sign the card, while someone else tries to collect $10 from every team member. All this ends with the team gathering around a coworker's cubicle to sing, "Happy Birthday," while slices of dry supermarket cake are served up on paper plates. This can get old after a while.

If birthdays are "Boardwalk" on the Monopoly board, then corporate birthdays can be likened to "Park Place." One way you can make a great impression as a manager is to recognize an employee's corporate birthday. Corporate birthdays are unique because you as the manager own the real estate. When was the last time you heard a coworker congratulate another coworker on being with the firm for three years? Employees don't do this because most of them do not feel it is their place. This spot is reserved for management. A simple acknowledgment of a corporate birthday is a great way to show that you care, and it gives you an opportunity to share something appreciative about the employee. No cake, card, or money collection is required and, thankfully, no one has to sing!

Happy Cinco de Mayo!

With the workplace becoming increasingly multicultural, another simple way to show you care is to take an interest in the cultural background of your direct reports. If you have someone on your staff who has emigrated from Mexico, you want to know that the 5th of May is a big holiday back home for them. During Cinco de Mayo, while your team member is working, family and friends back in Mexico are celebrating. To be able to pop your head into your employee's office and wish him or her, "Happy Cinco de Mayo," or to have the employee share what the holiday means to the rest of your team at the morning meeting will mean a lot. You could take it a step further and let them off work early. When you wish Rose, your employee from the Philippines, a "Happy Independence Day" on June 12, you cross over to Grandpa Jack's side of the street.

Lost in Translation

When I was leading a not-for-profit organization, we had a very diverse staff. From time to time, I would try to learn simple phrases in some of my staff members' native language. When you ask Tracy from Taiwan how to say, "Great work," and then a week later you tell her, "Great work," in Mandarin, she smiles, laughs at your awkward pronunciation, but appreciates the effort. Taking a genuine interest and learning from your direct reports communicates that you care about and respect them.

The key is to take small steps of *genuine* interest in your employees. Get started by discovering your employees' vital statistics and begin planning your weekly walkabout. It does not have to take a long time, but give it the same priority as you would a meeting with the CEO. Lastly, everything I have mentioned in this chapter is not to be viewed as management techniques. The goal is to take a genuine interest in your employees and show that you care. Feeling valued as individuals, those employees will be more inclined to become engaged and work harder. It's a win-win situation.

The Spouse Test

After speaking at a conference on the importance of taking a genuine interest in your employees, I had a manager approach me and tell me about the spouse test. It was an ingenious method he used to gauge whether or not his employees liked working for him. The spouse test, he explained, took place whenever he had a chance to meet one of his employees' significant others. This typically happened at the year-end holiday party. If a spouse of one of his employees was warm, accepting, and genuinely friendly toward him, he passed. If a spouse was reserved and even cool toward him, then he knew he might not be doing as well as he'd hoped. While not foolproof, the spouse test is a brilliant way to gauge how you are doing with your staff. The reason, of course, is that people tend to like those who care about their loved ones. Conversely, anytime that people feel that one of their loved ones is being used or taken advantage of, they are unimpressed. The spouse test acts as a sort of mirror of how you are really doing with your direct reports.

THE KEY QUESTION

At the end of each chapter you will find a short summary including key lessons, action steps, and a key question. *Nine Minutes on Monday* is founded on nine key questions to ask yourself each Monday morning during your leadership planning time. Each question is tied to one of the nine drivers of employee engagement and will help you create small actionable goals that will inspire and motivate your staff.

MINUTE ONE SUMMARY

Key Lessons

- Trust is influence.
- Trust springs from three sources:
  1. Character
  2. Competence
  3. Caring
- When employees feel that management takes a genuine interest in them as individuals, it drives engagement.

Key Question

- How will I take a genuine interest in my employees this week?

Key Action Steps

- Access the Nine Minutes on Monday Toolkit. Go to www.nineminutesonmonday.com and download the tool "Vital Statistics."
- Take one minute to think through your employees and schedule a walkabout to do one of the following:
  - Show an interest
  - Inquire about a burden
  - Celebrate a corporate birthday
  - Acknowledge a cultural event

• MINUTE 1 •

How will I take a genuine interest
in my employees this week?

Mountains, Not Treadmills
The Need for Mastery

It's not the mountains we conquer, but ourselves.

—Sir Edmund Hillary

Yᵒu tend to take it for granted that when you reach out to shake someone's hand, it will be there. The first time I met Paul, he extended his left hand, which promoted an awkward, upside down kind of handshake. It was then that I noticed the shiny prosthetic hook sticking out where his right hand should have been. Paul had lost his lower right arm while working on a garbage truck. While it would be natural to feel sorry for Paul's loss, he thinks otherwise. Instead of a disability, Paul sees his new hook as an enhancement. So much so that if he was offered a chance to miraculously have his hand back, he would politely decline.

During a conversation with my wife, he explained it this way. "Right now life is a challenge, and I have to figure out how to do everything in a new way. If I had two hands, life would be boring."

What is going on in the mind of a man who would rather give left-handed handshakes than return to the two-handed life he had before his accident? Research in the field of psychology can explain Paul's attitude. It appears that we all have a deep-seated need for something called mastery.

Mastery could be described as our desire to overcome a challenge.

In doing so, we find meaning and purpose. In fact, the strings of mastery are woven into every facet of our being. Almost every movie you watch is a story of mastery. There is a beginning, then some kind of struggle, and hopefully—if it's a Hollywood ending—a resolution or triumph during which the characters experience profound growth.

When George Mallory, the legendary mountaineer, was asked why he wanted to climb Mount Everest, his famous response was, "Because it's there."

Mallory may not have realized it at the time, but he was speaking of that invisible force within each of us that desires to test our limits and experience growth.

Every day on the playground this need for mastery plays out as four-year-old boys and girls climb too high, swing too fast, and find ways to turn a simple slide into their own Mt. Everest. Anxious mothers watch and shout words of caution from the sidelines—"That's too high, Jimmy!" "Use two hands, Mary!" Their words have little effect, however, because even in our earliest days we are driven to test, to expand, and to engage in a challenge.

Frederick Herzberg, whose research led him to develop the motivation hygiene theory back in the 1960s, concluded that one of the greatest motivators at work is our need for achievement. For many employees today, this need for mastery and achievement is often left unmet, resulting in a precious loss of natural motivation.

MOUNTAINS, NOT TREADMILLS

My brother is a manager at an environmental services company. For the most part he spends his day crunching data that he then passes on to someone else. Last summer he visited my parents, who had recently purchased a large 20-foot by 50-foot greenhouse. It came in a kit and needed to be assembled. This was no small project. My brother, however, was eager for the challenge and couldn't wait for the plane to land so he could get started.

I picked him up at the airport and delivered the bad news. "Dad already hired some guy to build the greenhouse."

My brother was visibly upset and said something to me that has stuck to this day: "All day long I analyze data and then pass it down the line. I just wanted to come and build something."

My brother was expressing his need for mastery. It was not being exercised at his work, so he was looking for another outlet to satisfy this longing. Why else would someone want to use his holiday to build a greenhouse? Perhaps for the very same reason that someone with one hand might never want to go back to living with two.

When I am conducting one of my leadership programs for a company, I always start by asking the managers in the room what they hope to get out of the day. This helps me get a feel for where the group is and helps me further tailor the program to fit their specific needs. Typically, about 70 percent of the group will tell me they want to know how to motivate people. This is understandable, and an important skill to be acquired by all who manage. I do provide tools to do this; however, one of the best ways to motivate your staff is to make their jobs more enriching by providing a sense of mastery and achievement. Many jobs in today's world are less like climbing mountains and more like running on a treadmill. A lot of energy is spent but little to no perceived progress is made. As a manger, you want your people climbing mountains instead of running on treadmills.

GO WITH THE FLOW

Mihaly Csíkszentmihályi (pronounced chick-sent-mee-high) has spent his life studying motivation. His research has shaped how we think about the art and science of motivating people. A large part of Csíkszentmihályi's work has centered around a principle he calls flow. *Flow* is a state of profound engagement where one loses oneself in a task. It is a highly self-motivated state typified by total absorption in the task, single-minded immersion, and spontaneous joy, causing time to pass by almost unnoticed. Sounds good, doesn't it? Flow states are common when we are engaged in things we love, such as our favorite hobbies. However, Mihaly Csíkszentmihályi's research found that people actually experience more flow states during work than during their own recreational time. This is good news for managers.

So how do you get your employees into this highly engaged state? Flow states are a bit like tornados. You cannot really force them to happen, yet there are certain conditions under which they tend to occur. The great news is that, as a manager, you have a lot of influence over creating the optimal conditions in which flow states are more likely to appear. This is important because it means that you can increase your staff's engagement by creating optimal conditions for flow in the workplace. When flow states arise, they end up doing the heavy lifting with respect to motivation. When the job itself provides the fuel for your staff, you do not have to work hard to engage them. So what are the conditions necessary for flow? Flow states arise when there are clear goals or expectations, when these goals are optimally challenging, and when there is some system of immediate and consistent feedback.

CLEAR GOALS AND EXPECTATIONS

My wife is a nutritionist and a personal trainer. Our garage has been converted into a private training studio with everything you need to get ripped abs and bulging biceps. Do I have six-pack abs? Not quite. Actually, not by a long shot. Truth is, even with all the equipment and the gym being in my own house and a wife showing me what I should eat, I had not been working out because I simply wasn't motivated. Sure, I could have slugged my way through a couple of workouts because I felt guilty or by using pure will power. But these would have led to half-hearted and ineffective workouts. Everything changed, however, when I decided to commit to a climbing expedition to Aconcagua in Argentina. Aconcagua is one of the world's seven summits and is the highest peak in the western hemisphere. It demands that you be in premiere shape to climb it. I had decided to try the Polish Glacier route and, with deposit now paid, I found myself back in the gym, pushing myself, working hard, and quickly getting into shape.

My motivation suddenly changed because I now had a goal that required me to be in shape. The motivation was not necessarily in the goal itself; it was spurred by the gap that the goal created. Gaps create unpleasant feelings of incongruity, which motivate us to act in order to alleviate some of the discomfort. Now that I had a deadline for a certain place I needed to be, I was able to look at where I was, and the difference between the two (which was vast) motivated me to begin closing the gap.

We like to know where we are and where we need to go, while the size of the gap in between the two provides us feedback on what we have to do next.

Clear goals and expectations also provide structure. Structure is important because when employees know exactly what is required of them, they experience a sense of security. This security reduces the stress caused by ambiguity. Freshly motivated for my Aconcagua expedition, I realized that my wife's workout plan provided a structure for me that removed the uncertainty of what I should be doing. By removing choices and options, I was able to pursue the goal with more resources and dedication.

Last, goals elevate performance. Because goals challenge us to move beyond where we are, they result in our trying harder, which, in turn, leads to improved performance. The fact that goals result in improved performance is one of the most replicable findings in all psychological research. Goals also result in greater persistence, especially in the face of obstacles. They often inspire us to come up with new ways to reach our target in the face of challenges, causing us to succeed where we may have previously given up.

When it comes to goal setting, the secret is in how it is done. The most important aspects of goals that lead to flow are ones that are both specific and challenging. In fact, there are over 100 published studies on the power of goals that are both specific and challenging. Specific goals direct and focus behaviors, while challenging goals engage and amplify effort.

OPTIMAL BALANCE—HARD BUT NOT TOO HARD

While challenging goals increase effort, goals that are too challenging actually diminish it. The secret is in creating optimal challenge. As Jim, Osvaldo, and I rested at 20,000 feet, we still had almost 1,500 vertical feet to climb before we reached the summit. We had begun the day with a specific and challenging goal, but as we chewed into it, Jim and I realized that it might be too big for either of us. We were both struggling to believe that we could do it. When the seeds of doubt sprout in your mind, they begin to suck dry any remaining pools of motivation. Osvaldo, our guide, sat in silence, weighing the options. After a few moments he looked up and said, "You see that ridge up there?"

Jim and I looked upward toward the summit and spotted the ridge.

"Let's stop there," Osvaldo continued. "It will take us only about 45 minutes."

While I was not thrilled about another 45 minutes of climbing upward, I was at least excited to have the end within sight. Jim and I looked at each other and nodded in agreement. "Okay," we agreed.

Moments later we were climbing again, but now with renewed energy. For hours we had been trudging along making very slow progress toward a peak we could not see. Often on a mountain, the summit is obscured from your view. This can be very demoralizing. The same thing can happen when individuals cannot see their end point or when their goal is simply too big. Without milestones to break the goal down into manageable sections, motivation will often wane. By having us focus on the ridge, Osvaldo was, in fact, breaking the mountain down into something more manageable, something that we believed we could do.

Csíkszentmihályi found that in order for an activity to elicit a flow state, there had to be the right balance between the challenge of the task at hand and the skills and abilities of the individual faced with performing the task. Goals that are too challenging fail to engage and motivate because deep down people don't actually believe they can achieve them. In other words, if the gap between where they are and where they need to be is too wide, it will not result in motivated effort. Part of the reason for this is self-protection. Why would we want to expend ourselves fully only to fail? Such things are hard on our egos. This is often seen in sales, where managers set ridiculously high sales goals for their employees thinking it will motivate them to try harder. If the goal is too big—that is, if it's beyond the employees' belief that it can be accomplished—then they will withhold their best efforts and subsequently fall miserably short. On the other hand, tasks that are too easy do not inspire engagement either because no real exertion is required. Tasks that are too easy have the potential to incite boredom and apathy, both of which are detrimental to high performance. So in order to create situations that are ideal for a flow state, you must strike the balance of hard, but not too hard.

Csíkszentmihályi demonstrated this balance in the diagram in Figure 2, where the vertical axis represents the scale of difficulty of the task and the horizontal axis represents the skill level of the individual. Notice that there is an optimal area, called the flow channel, where the challenge of the task matches the skill of the employee. Inside this zone, people are in optimal conditions for flow. In other words, there is balance between how hard a task is and how skilled the employee is. If the task, however, becomes increasingly difficult without any increase in skills (shown by moving straight up on the graph), the employee will feel a great deal of anxiety. Imagine someone asking you to give a speech to 1,000 people with only two hours' notice. Unless you are used to this, the mere thought will likely get your heart racing.

On the other hand, if an employee is increasing in skills without having an opportunity to work on something more challenging (represented by moving straight to the right on the graph), then the task is bound to result in boredom. Neither of these states—anxiety or boredom—leads to engagement and fulfilling work.

Joan has been working at an advertising company for about a year. She has settled in nicely and enjoys the work. For the last six months she has been able to work with some of the senior designers, helping them create marketing campaigns for clients. Once there is an initial concept and design, the ideas are then presented to the client in the company's boardroom. One day Joan's boss approaches her and asks her to deliver the presentation on the McGavin account. Joan has never done this before and immediately feels a rush of anxiety.

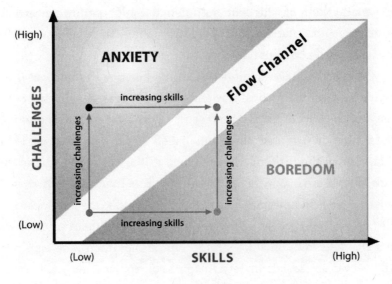

Figure 2

Anxiety, boredom, and flow (Csíkszentmihályi, 1990)

Source: ©Trevor van Gorp, 2006 (captions added)

In Figure 3 we have just moved Joan from A to B. Notice that the increase in the challenge has taken Joan out of a flow state and into anxiety's territory. With the determination to do it, along with a lot of reassurance from her boss, Joan dives into the challenge. She pulls off the presentation and does well enough that her boss wants her to do more. With each presentation, Joan gains skills and experience. As she does this, she moves from B to C on the flow diagram. Notice that after some training and experience she is back in a state of flow (C). This is a great place for Joan because she enjoys a balance between the challenge of the task and her newly acquired skills.

As the months go by, Joan continues to make presentations to clients with great success. After a while, however, the task becomes too easy for her and eventually fails to challenge her at all. Joan has now moved from C to D on the diagram and into boredom's territory. Notice that Joan has left the flow channel for this task. She still does a great job, but it no longer engages her the way it used to. Joan is craving something more challenging, which will take her from D back up

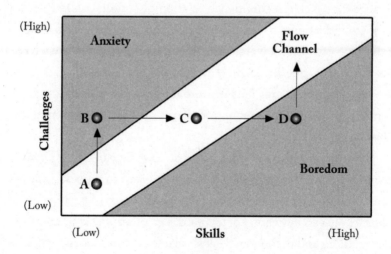

Figure 3

An example of employee progression through flow states

into the flow channel again. If Joan is not able to take on something that will stretch her abilities, she will eventually tire of her job and be tempted to look for something new. Csíkszentmihályi's work on flow has given us a powerful visual to help us understand the relationship between challenging work, skill acquisition, and engagement. Your people are most engaged when they are performing work that is optimally challenging.

How do you know whether a task is optimally challenging? As Csíkszentmihályi discovered, the difficulty of a task has very little to do with its actual difficulty. Both the level of difficulty and the skill level of the individual are largely based on their own perception. It doesn't matter if the task is easy to everyone else on the team; if one of your employees feels it is beyond his skill level (whether it is or not), it will produce anxiety. In order to create the optimal challenge for an employee, a manager must take into account the beliefs of her direct reports. This is where you can have an enormous impact on your employees by helping them adjust their view of their own abilities.

Many people are held back from reaching their potential simply because they lack the confidence to attempt certain challenges. They carry around a belief of inadequacy that hinders them from engaging in the type of work they are capable of. Managers sometimes have to play the role of cheerleader, helping people see their skills and abilities for what they really are. This is more than simple encouragement, as there is a direct link to perception of abilities and higher motivation states such as flow.

How do you maximize conditions of flow? One of the ways you can do this is by involving employees in the goal-setting process. This helps them not only to feel a sense of ownership but also to find that critical balance between hard and not too hard. The other way is by continually helping them add to their skill set so that their confidence in their own proficiency will continue to grow. Of course, it's not just about helping them grow; helping employees see their growth also plays a critical role in motivating them to take on increasingly difficult challenges. It is a delicate art to be able to stretch employees just enough to engage them and mobilize that extra effort, but not to where they pass the point of what they think is possible. However, even with clear goals that are optimally challenging, the key ingredient to maximizing the possibility of a flow state is consistent and immediate feedback.

ARE WE THERE YET? THE POWER OF CONSISTENT FEEDBACK

One of the most terrifying experiences for a human being is the feeling of being lost. You might have first experienced it as a child when you couldn't find your mother in the department store after you had wandered off. We are a species that likes to have our bearings. Knowing where we are gives us security.

This aversion to being lost goes beyond the physical, and touches almost every other area of our lives. We use phrases like, "Where do I stand in this company?" or, "How am I doing in this course?" Knowing where we are is essential because it helps us know how to feel and what to do next.

Humans crave feedback. If you have ever decided to save money and drive your kids to Disneyland (something you do only once), you will constantly be bombarded with the recurring question, "Are we there yet?" Trying to explain to a four-year-old that you still have 120 miles to go is a challenge, especially when the child has not yet grasped the concept of time. So you find creative ways to give feedback and say something like, "By the time you watch one more movie, we will be there."

This feedback is important to the child because it helps him or her know how to feel and what to do next, which is—hopefully—sleep.

The workplace can sometimes seem like riding in the back of your parent's car on a long trip. It's hard to know where you are or how long it will take for you to reach your destination (if there even is one) when you don't have the information in a form that means something to you. When there is no meaningful feedback, there is little possibility of nurturing the need for mastery.

FEEDBACK MOTIVATES

Have you ever been to a family reunion or similar type of gathering, and someone has set up a volleyball net? Everyone is politely hitting the ball back and forth over the net just having fun and not keeping score. This can go on for only so long until people grow bored. While it may be fun in the beginning, it soon loses its sense of challenge. Then Uncle Willy, while fetching the ball from under Aunt Edna's lawn chair, suggests, "Let's play for real." Suddenly, with those four simple words, everything changes. People start diving for the ball, arguments break out over whether the last serve was in or out, and teammates admonish one another to "call the ball." How did this civilized family-friendly activity of bumping a ball over a net turn into a motivated and spirited game of elite athletes? What changed? It is the same ball, the same net, and even the same people. The difference is feedback. We introduced a system of feedback we call "keeping score," and it provided a measure that helped us regulate our actions.

When employees have clear goals that strike the right balance between challenge and skill, and you introduce a system for ongoing and immediate feedback, highly energized and motivated flow states are set to emerge.

Feedback is one of the most important tools in a manager's tool kit and yet one that is not put to work nearly enough. Your employees crave feedback. They want to know how they are doing, where they are doing well, and where they could be doing better. Feedback is the magic sauce that gives power to goals. Because people are inherently poor at evaluating their own performance, they look to outside cues for help. If there are no clear and specific goals to paint this picture for them, then they must rely on the subjective input of their manager and their own (often flawed) estimation. When employees work day in and day out without a sense of knowing where they stand, it erodes self-motivation and has the potential to leave them feeling insecure about their performance.

Feedback is not only for when things are going poorly. It reminds me of the old joke where a wife complains to her husband that he never says, "I love you," any more, and he responds with, "I told you I loved you on our wedding day, and if anything changes, I'll let you know." Some managers resemble the miserly husband doling out feedback only for times when things need to be improved. Start viewing feedback as information. Sometimes it tells your employees that they need to do better; other times it says that they are going above and beyond, or that they're right where they need to be. Whichever one, at least they know where they stand.

The best companies know the power of feedback and schedule it accordingly. Recently I was flipping through a magazine that highlighted the top 100 companies to work for in my city. As I read through some of the summaries, one thing stood out. Many of the companies had made conscious efforts to provide above-average amounts of scheduled feedback for their employees. While scheduled feedback such as performance reviews are great, nothing beats what I call guerrilla feedback. These are the unscheduled, impromptu moments where you drop in on your direct reports to let them know how they are doing. It may consist of nothing more than a sentence or two, but it helps them feel secure and knowledgeable about where they stand.

It's in the Numbers

In his book *The Three Signs of a Miserable Job*, Patrick Lencioni highlights immeasurability as a major problem in today's work environment. Jobs that cannot be measured numerically make it hard for people to know how they are doing. While not possible for every job, finding a way to measure progress numerically is powerful. Numbers give people a yardstick that is objective. "You've produced 100 widgets," is concrete, whereas, "You are doing your job up to standards," is vague and sub-jective. As humans we like things in concrete terms, so whenever pos-sible, try to find ways to measure certain areas of performance. This can sometimes take extra thought and creativity. Lencioni's book is an excellent source for ideas.

In occupations in which it is difficult to measure anything, you as a manager must fill the void by providing feedback on your employ-ees' performance on a consistent basis. In such scenarios, try to be as specific as you can. For instance, let's say that you happened to walk by Mary while she was on the phone with a customer, and you liked the way she handled the call. You might give her some feedback such as, "Mary, I overheard your call to a customer this morning. The way you explained their options was very clear and succinct. If you do that with every caller, you can know you are doing an exceptional job." Some might call this recognition, and others may call it coaching. And in some ways it's both. But more than that, it's information that helps Mary know what success looks like, and this is the essential ingredient. When employees know what success in their role looks like, it not only motivates them, but it also assists you when you're attempting to give specific feedback. Success is not always defined in numerical terms. A lot of times it is more the result of a set of behaviors, outcomes, and even attitudes strung together over time. By identifying what they are, you are setting yourself up to improve the effectiveness of your feedback.

GPS and Altimeters

When you are climbing in the mountains, the lead guide will often have a global positioning system, or GPS. This tells the guide your exact coordinates on the mountain as well as how high you are. It also provides feedback on the path taken and how far off the intended path your party may be.

The rest of the climbers in the party may not have a GPS but most will carry some kind of altimeter, usually on their watch. The altimeter measures altitude. It will not tell you exactly where you are, but it at least registers how high up the mountain you've climbed. So if your next camp is at 20,000 feet and your altimeter reads 19,500 feet, you know that you have 500 vertical feet to ascend before you can stop for the day. This ability for climbers to self-measure is important. It saves them from having to keep asking the lead guide, "Are we there yet?" Being able to self-measure also helps climbers make their own personal adjustments, whether it's managing their energy or rationing their food and water consumption.

When employees have concrete goals that can be measured numerically or checkpoints that they must reach that are well defined, it gives them a way to self-measure. It's like giving them their own altimeter to provide feedback, which will help their own engagement.

Leaning Golf Course Pins

When I was a teenager working at the golf course, one of my jobs was to change the pin placement every day. This involved digging a new hole and filling in the old one. To my boss's credit, he taught me exactly what success looked like on this particular job. When I was finished, the key indicators were whether or not the new pin was standing up straight as opposed to leaning to the side, and whether or not the grass plug I used to fill in the previous hole blended in seamlessly. While there was not much to measure numerically, I was crystal clear on what success looked like. I still remember driving around the golf course later in the day, glancing occasionally at the flag poles on each hole, each one commending me or nudging me to do better next time. Either way, I had feedback.

Turning Treadmills into Mountains

Earlier I said that you want your people to climb mountains and not run on treadmills. But can we turn treadmills into mountains? Let's look at an actual treadmill for a moment. Spending 30 minutes on a treadmill can be incredibly agonizing because of the sheer boredom.

What if we applied the principles of flow to our workout? Imagine that you are a personal trainer and your job is to motivate people to do their treadmill session. Instead of simply telling them to run for 30 minutes, you could set a goal for them to keep their heart rate in the red zone for at least 28 minutes. You could also plan three intense one-minute sprints, each at a speed of 10 miles per hour during the workout, and from the twenty-fifth minute mark until the twenty-ninth minute mark the treadmill will be ramped up to a 15 percent incline. Last, you tell your clients that every time they want to say, "I can't do this," they are instead going to say, "I *can* do this."

Already your clients will be enticed by the mountain you have created before them and will be eager to get started. In this example we have created some clear goals that are optimally challenging, and we have numerous channels of immediate feedback. These are the conditions in which flow states occur. Motivation for the workout no longer has to come from you because now the job itself (the treadmill workout) will be doing the heavy lifting in terms of keeping your clients motivated.

Any Given Sunday

Shane volunteers at his church, faithfully lugging heavy sound equipment to a rented school cafeteria every Sunday where he sets it up for the worship service. If you wanted to make sure that Shane was climbing mountains instead of running treadmills, what might you do? The first thing would be to help Shane define what success looks like in his role. Pulling him into this conversation is a wise idea, because it will help him feel more ownership for the responsibility. This conversation will likely result in the creation of some kind of list consisting of certain behaviors and attitudes that he needs to help pull off a successful service. It may contain items such as:

- Show up by 9:30 a.m.
- Use duct tape to secure all wires.

- Adjust microphone stand heights so singers don't have to do it.
- Speak with song team to find out if there are any special arrangements.
- Adjust volumes to correct level according to each speaker.
- Test wireless microphone to ensure that there is no feedback.
- Respond cheerfully if a child interrupts his work.

Even though this is a volunteer position at a church on Sunday, this clarity of expectations will help Shane know how he is doing. This also makes it easier for the minister to give Shane feedback on his performance. Instead of Shane carrying on his duties in the background, he now has a better chance of experiencing a sense of achievement on any given Sunday.

When we combine clear expectations—which properly balance skill and difficulty—with a system of continual feedback, we help meet an employee's deep psychological need for mastery. When people experience mastery, they will be more engaged, productive, and ultimately happier at work. As a manager, spend some time thinking through each of your direct reports' weekly roles and responsibilities. Do they have clear goals and expectations? Do these goals challenge and stretch them? And last, is there a way for them to receive feedback regarding their progress? The quickest way to know whether your people are climbing mountains or running on treadmills is whether you can give them feedback or not. If you cannot give feedback to one of your employees on her progress in any given week, chances are she is on a treadmill. That's why, during your leadership planning time, your second minute is to ponder one simple question: Whom will I give feedback to this week? Pick an employee and let him know how he is doing.

MINUTE TWO SUMMARY

Key Lessons

- Mastery is our need to engage in our environment, struggle with a challenge, and overcome.
- Make jobs more engaging by creating conditions of flow.
- Flow states occur when there are clear goals or expectations, optimal challenges, and consistent feedback.

Key Question

- Whom will I give feedback to this week?

Key Action Step

- Go to www.nineminutesonmonday.com and download the "Mountains and Mastery" worksheet.

• MINUTE 2 •

Whom will I give feedback to
this week?

The Midas Touch
The Need for Recognition

A prince should be slow to punish and quick to reward.

—Ovid

If you find yourself buried beneath rubble during an earthquake or under three feet of snow after an avalanche, you had better hope that the search and rescue dog looking for you is highly motivated. Search and rescue (SAR) dogs need about 600 hours of training before they are ready to work in the field, and not just any dog is cut out for the job. Among other traits, such as obedience and focus, a good candidate to become a SAR dog is one that possesses a strong drive to hunt for a tossed toy and has a strong desire to please.

While lying trapped beneath three feet of rubble, imagine your joy when you hear the muffled barking of a SAR dog above you. As the rescuers make their way down to you, sunlight suddenly streams through an opening in the debris. While you might expect to be greeted by the sniffing nose of the SAR dog, this is often not the case. Chances are he has already moved on to a friendly game of tug-of-war between his handler and a smelly sock. Even though this accident scene seems hardly the place to be playing around, the dog and his handler are acting out an important ritual. The dog is being rewarded for finding you. This is necessary in motivating the SAR dog to want to look for more people.

In fact, without these small moments of reward and recognition, a SAR dog may even give up and stop working altogether. For the person still buried beneath the rubble somewhere, this is bad news.

As much as we like to think we've evolved far beyond the animal kingdom, rewards and recognition have a powerful effect on our behavior as well. They are, in fact, crucial pieces in the motivation puzzle. Few concepts carry as much power or have as much potential for influencing behavior as simple reward and recognition.

INCREASED MOTIVATION

Reward and recognition act as a source of fuel, which can stir employees to try harder, persist longer in the face of difficulty, and invest more energy. Have you ever doubled your efforts in order to qualify for a year-end bonus? Or have you ever put that extra touch on a project because you wanted your boss to be pleased with it? We are hard-wired for reward and recognition. Part of the reason is biological. Whenever we receive praise or recognition, our brain releases dopamine, a neurotransmitter in the brain in charge of stimulating our pleasure centers. Dopamine is also behind many of the temporary highs resulting from addictive substances such as cocaine.

Shapes Behavior

Managers must shape and promote effective behavior in order to produce results. Managers can increase the frequency of any behavior by properly applying reward and recognition. It has been said, "What is rewarded gets repeated." Again we see dopamine at work as its temporary high links behavior with reward. This is why positive reinforcement works so well.

Builds Trust

When you consistently appreciate and recognize your employees, it strengthens the bonds of goodwill, which are essential for building trust. Recognizing good work and effort shows that you appreciate and value people for who they are and what they do. This type of gratitude promotes trust which, as you know, is the currency of leadership.

Provides Feedback
Reward and recognition also act as a form of feedback that helps your employees know how they are doing. When employees are exceeding expectations, feedback can be given in the form of praise and recognition. Feedback, as mentioned earlier, is what we rely on to help us know how to feel, how to act, and how to adjust.

So with all these benefits, why don't managers do a better job of rewarding and recognizing their staff? In a study of 65 potential incentives in the workplace, conducted by Dr. Gerald Graham of Wichita State University, the most motivating incentive was simply a manager who "personally congratulates an employee for doing a good job." However, 58 percent of the respondents said their manager rarely—if ever—offered such simple praise. Graham concluded, "It appears that the techniques that have the greatest motivational impact are practiced the least, even though they are easier and less expensive to use."

Picking up a management book that does not include a chapter on recognition and appreciation is like picking up Mother Teresa's diary and not finding the word "prayer." Yet, even with this common knowledge, vast numbers of employees still feel that they are underappreciated for their efforts. Why the disconnect?

In all my dealings with managers, there are a few common reasons why reward and recognition are not practiced more regularly. Here are the six most common reasons why managers don't excel at reward and recognition:

1. *I'm too busy:* It is not that we are bad people or that we don't appreciate what our employees do. For most of us, it's a simple case of being too busy to think about it. Like the pilots on Eastern Airlines, we get

consumed in the details around us and forget to look up and give attention to some of the more important issues. In fact, the hectic pace that most managers operate under make it easy to go an entire week and fail to see what was good or praiseworthy around them.

2. *They are simply doing their job:* Why should I reward or appreciate employees for doing what they are paid to do? While this mindset seems to be fading, it still exists. Some managers feel that appreciation is found in an employee's paycheck. This might work for robots, but since we depend on people to bring their best to work in order to produce results, we need to find ways to reinforce excellent behaviors.

3. *No one is recognizing me:* It is easy to neglect the practice of rewarding and recognizing employees when we ourselves are not being valued by our superiors. In these situations, rewarding our employees can sometimes stir feelings of injustice. But true leaders are the ones who do what is right regardless of what may be happening to them. Great leaders rise above and break the unhealthy cycle so as not to propagate further leadership incompetence.

4. *I don't want to show favoritism:* Some managers have told me they do not want to show favoritism. This view stems from their people-pleasing nature and does not inspire a workplace of excellence. Why should you punish great effort by failing to recognize it for the sake of those who are not performing? This desire not to offend anyone is a sure way to sabotage the high performers while rewarding mediocrity. One of the best safeguards against favoritism is to make sure you are spreading reward and recognition around. More on this later in the chapter.

5. *We already have an employee recognition program:* Some managers assume that it is the organization's duty to reward great performances. While this is important, one survey found that 57 percent of employees would rather hear praise from their direct supervisor as opposed to 21 percent who would rather hear it from senior management. When it comes to recognition of your employees, your

voice carries more weight than the CEO's. Bob Nelson, an expert on employee recognition, found that managers who excelled at rewarding and recognizing their employees did so in part because they saw it as their personal responsibility.

6. *I'm not sure how:* I had one manager say to me, "You can only say thank you so many times before it loses its meaning." While he did have a point, he was missing an important concept. Reward and recognition is not about saying thank you (although that's a good place to start). It's more about helping people feel valued. What this manager needed was more tools in his toolbox on how to help his employees feel appreciated. The phrases "thank you" and "great job" are fine starters, but on their own they have limited impact.

The Need to Be Valued

Reward and recognition help meet a fundamental need deep within each of us. It's really more the answer to a question. We all want to know if we are needed, if we are significant, if we are valuable. Since we often attach what we do or produce to who we are, we tend to think that if people value and appreciate what we do, then they most likely appreciate and value us as people as well. If you want to transform your proficiency at rewarding and recognizing your employees, then begin by viewing it as a way to help your people feel valuable.

Refrigerator Pictures—The Value Proposition

Let's go back in time for a moment. Remember when you were four or five years old? Your agenda was fairly simple. The only real commitments you had were possibly *Sesame Street* at 11:00 a.m. and maybe an afternoon nap at around 2:00 p.m. No doubt you owned a pack of crayons and, depending on what generation you are from, it probably contained anywhere between 8 crayons (Baby Boomers), all the way up to 128 crayons with the built-in sharpener (if you are a Generation Y). Unable to play outside because of the rain, you set out to create a masterpiece. With your tongue sticking out of the side of your mouth, you focused all your attention and energy on the white sheet of paper in front of you. It was engaging, it was intrinsic, and it was fun. But after the initial satisfaction of completing your picture, you realized there was still one thing left to do. You had to show it to someone. After all, you had worked hard and you thought it was a good picture, but you still needed outside validation. The obvious choice was usually your mother. As you presented it to her, you studied her face to see what she thought. Of course, a smile always broke out across her face as she showered you and your creation with admiring praise. The final confirmation that this was truly a work of art was whether it would be put on display for public viewing. Back then you didn't know about the Louvre in Paris or the National Gallery in London, but you had something equally prestigious for any aspiring artist—the refrigerator door. Even then you understood that there was a powerful link between what you created and how you felt about yourself. You did not realize it at the time, but your mother had just given you the Midas touch.

THE MIDAS TOUCH

When the Greek god Bacchus granted King Midas a wish, the king asked that everything he touched would be turned to gold. Initially, this seemed like a great idea as stones and twigs transformed to gold under his fingertips. Yet, when King Midas touched his own daughter and she became a statue, he realized that his gift was actually a curse.

We are intrigued by the story of King Midas because, after all, who wouldn't want to turn simple objects into gold, as long as we could turn off this ability when appropriate? Need money for your mortgage payment? Here, touch this tin can!

A similar power is at our fingertips when it comes to those we lead. The Midas touch can turn your people into gold. It can make them feel valuable for who they are and what they do, and this is an important part of the engagement equation.

Throughout this chapter I have used the terms reward *and* recognition. While each one has the same end goal, they differ greatly in their impact and how they are implemented. Rewarding someone usually involves giving them something tangible—cash, gift certificates, trophies, certificates, and so on. Recognition, on the other hand, usually involves intangibles such as words of praise. While both can be effective, I try to steer managers away from giving out rewards and encourage them to opt for simple recognition instead. There are several reasons for this. First, rewards can actually hinder long-term performance by undermining intrinsic motivation. You will learn more about this in Chapter 9 on autonomy. Second, because rewards are usually reserved for those extra special above-and-beyond types of performances, they are usually few and far between. If a manager solely relies on these to help her people feel valuable and appreciated, she will miss out on hundreds of other smaller opportunities to motivate her staff. While there definitely is a place for tangible rewards, be sure to use them with discretion. Because so much of the "value" is connected to the tangible reward, picking the appropriate item can be a challenge. "So I gave up my weekends for a month to finish this project, and they give me a coffee mug with our company logo on it? Gee, thanks!"

Because individuals value things differently, this adds to the challenge of determining what type of reward is actually rewarding: "We know Jim doesn't golf, but the putter we're giving him might motivate him to take up the sport."

There also seems to be a difference between cash and noncash rewards. In fact, when it comes to cash rewards, the research suggests that you skip them. As much as people always want more money, it actually makes for a lousy reward. In one study, even though almost eight out of ten people said they would rather have a cash incentive as motivation for playing a word game, their performance improved from 15 to over 38 percent when a noncash incentive was introduced. Clearly, they misunderstood their own preference for performance incentives.

Another study comparing cash and noncash rewards as an incentive for increasing car sales revealed that noncash rewards increased sales by 15 percent compared to 2 percent for cash.

Another problem with cash rewards is their usefulness. One survey found that the majority of cash reward recipients didn't spend the money on anything memorable. Because cash rewards are often used to pay down things like credit card debt, the reward seems to evaporate with little or nothing tangible or meaningful to show for it.

Another related problem with cash as a reward is our quandary about how to spend it. In one study, 70 percent of people felt it would not be justifiable to spend their bonus money on something self-satisfying, like a trip. This is understandable, especially if the employee has any type of outstanding debt such as a credit card balance. Compare that with a noncash reward like travel. The trip comes with anticipation, the experience itself, and the memories to take home after it's over. In fact, some research suggests that noncash rewards such as trips stimulate the right side of the brain, resulting in more goal imagery and therefore activating more motivation channels in our brain. The last problem with rewards is that because many of them cost money, they are often beyond the decision-making power of the manager. This usually results in a complicated jumble of hoops for the manager to jump through just to secure two movie tickets for one employee.

Fortunately, giving your employees recognition does not have to be complicated or expensive. When it comes to helping your people feel like gold, there are three general areas that will give you the most bang for your buck in the workplace. They are: recognizing achievements, recognizing behaviors, and recognizing personal attributes.

Recognizing Achievements

One day when I was seven years old, I discovered a powerful combination when I was out behind the barn. I learned that if you add a gallon of gasoline to a small flame, the results were—well—explosive! My best friend and I had filled an old ice cream pail full of gasoline and were having a great time exploring the field of pyrotechnics. Our experiment went suddenly wrong after I decided to pour the entire pail of gasoline on the tiny fire I had started. After spending my entire summer holidays in the burn ward and causing untold amounts of stress to my family, I had finally learned the incredible power of mixing tractor fuel with fire. Our world is filled with examples of other powerful pairings from the outright dangerous to the harmless glow stick that entertains children for hours as the chemicals combine for a reaction inside a small plastic tube.

Frederick Herzberg's ground-breaking research on motivation in the 1960s led him to discover two powerful motivators which, when combined, have the potential for explosive results. These motivators were the desire to achieve and recognition and appreciation for that achievement. The two concepts, when combined, have the same energy-producing potential as the match and gasoline experiment I was involved in as a seven year old. This incredible link between recognition and our achievements has been woven into our DNA. For managers, we can leverage this history and tap into its incredible motivational properties.

At the end of every week your staff will have achieved any number of things—some big, most small. Each one of these achievements is a potential opportunity for you to exercise the Midas touch. Did they finish a report? Complete their project ahead of schedule? Come up with a new idea? Reach a goal? Hit a sales target? Whatever their achievement was, we want them to feel that it was valuable, and we also want them to feel valued.

Recognizing Behaviors

As a manager, you are actually in the business of managing behavior. By encouraging and promoting effective behaviors, you shape the environment that will lead your team to success. Reward and recognition is the force that reinforces those effective behaviors. Of course, this all begins by your having a crystal clear picture of what behaviors are required among your staff members. Once you know what you are looking for, you can then go about the task of reinforcing these behaviors through reward or recognition. As a manager, it is easy to slip into the mode of constant correction; you see what needs to be done better and you address it. While this is an essential part of management, it must be balanced with recognition of behaviors that are good. A great habit to get into is to make regular rounds among your staff, attempting to catch them doing something right. Every day in your office there are more good things that happen than there are bad. So leave the police officer's badge in your desk drawer and find someone exhibiting a behavior that you want to see again. What gets rewarded gets repeated.

Recognizing Attributes

While recognizing and rewarding people for what they do is essential, we also want to be sure that we appreciate and value them for who they are. This meets a deep need in all of us, as we inwardly struggle to know that our lives are significant. Instead of valuing only the report that your employee, John, created, you want to value something about John that led to the report being created. Was it his work ethic, his creativity, his attention to detail, or something else? These attributes need to be the target of much of our praise. By highlighting employees' personal qualities and characteristics, you place value on them as people.

While recognition of achievements, behaviors, and attributes can be powerful, the key is in how it's done. Reward and recognition is most effective when it's specific, timely, and done in such a way as to not rob people of their intrinsic motivation.

Why Do You Love Me?

One day recently, my phone beeped to inform me that I had a new text message. It was from my wife, and it simply said, "I love you." You might think that we are newlyweds still basking in the glow of honeymoon bliss, but we have been married close to 20 years. Although we have a close relationship, this text message seemed to come out of the blue, leaving me to wonder if something was up. So I texted back one simple word: "Why?"

You might laugh and suggest that we see a marriage counselor, but I can assure you that we are very much in love. I just wanted to know why, at 10:30 in the morning, she felt compelled to express her feelings about me.

While we don't go around sending our direct reports text messages and e-mails saying we love them, we often do something quite similar when we say things like, "You did a good job," or, "Great work," or the equally generic, "Way to go." While each of these is an expression of appreciation and recognition, each falls short because it fails to answer the question "why?" The "why" is important because it gives us something tangible to hold onto instead of relying on subjective expressions that lack punch, such as, "Good work."

My wife, upon receiving my text, immediately responded with, "Because you put up with me when I am in a bad mood, you help with the dishes, and you work hard for our family."

Of the two messages she sent, which one do you think made me feel better? Which text encouraged me more and made me feel—well—loved? Of course, the one that outlined what I did and who I am as a person. While the "I love you" text meant something to her because she knew the specifics, it lost some of its impact when communicated because it lacked the details behind the emotion. The more specifically appreciation is expressed, the more powerful its effect on the receiver.

The same is true of reward and recognition. It must be specific. As a manager, try to ban from your vocabulary such phrases as, "Great job," and, "Keep up the good work," unless they are used in conclusion of some specific recognition. Such phrases are too vague and miss out on the reinforcing power that the Midas touch is capable of.

Happy Belated

Forgetting a birthday is an awful feeling. Fortunately for us we have a phrase for such times. We can wish our friend a happy belated birthday. The only problem with belated birthday wishes is that they have a time limit. Like a coupon at the grocery store, they tend to expire—somewhere around the seven-day mark. Wishing someone a happy belated birthday a month after their actual birthday is a bit pathetic. Opportunities for reward and recognition are like birthdays; they have a short window before they are gone. Unless you catch it within the week, it's often too late to have any lasting effect. Praising Mary about her role in the board meeting that took place over a month ago will have minimal effect. You may even have to remind Mary of what it was she did to deserve your praise. The closer that recognition follows the actual occurrence, the more powerful it will be. The only place this rule does not apply is when you're recognizing an employee's attributes. Because this type of recognition does not hinge on a particular event, achievement, or behavior displayed, it can be used at any time. Recognizing and rewarding quickly is something that simply takes a bit of practice and an increased awareness of what is happening.

Leverage the Power of Cause and Effect

We live in a world of cause and effect. When people see how their actions impact and contribute to something larger than themselves, it gives more meaning and motivation to those actions. Whenever you recognize or appreciate people for what they have done or who they are, be sure to link it to a positive consequence.

In the workplace, most of our actions will have an impact on at least one of five different areas:

1. The company
2. The team
3. You, the boss

4. The customer
5. The employee

When you can help people see how their behavior or achievements affect one of the above areas, it multiplies the effect of the encouragement.

Let's conclude this chapter with a few examples to illustrate what we have discussed.

Your employee, Sally, has just finished a market research report on a potential new service your company is considering adding to its existing line of products. The report is impressive—illuminating and thorough. It's obvious that Sally has put a lot of time and effort into this. You can:

1. Do nothing because Sally is only doing what she is paid to do.
2. Stop by her office and say, "Sally, great job on the report. Thanks for doing this." While this is better than saying nothing at all, it lacks the punch a more detailed recognition statement can provide.
3. Give Sally some specific reward and recognition that will show that you value what she has created while linking it to a tangible consequence (the company, the team, you, the customer, or Sally herself).

For example: "Sally, I wanted to thank you for the work you did on the market research report. It was very detailed and thorough, and I know that's because of your keen eye for detail and ability to spot trends. And I just wanted to add that with a report like this it really helps our company know whether or not we should go ahead with this new venture. Without this, we would be walking in blind. Your report is helping us see. Thanks for doing such an excellent job."

Do you see how we recognized her by, first, valuing the report (it was detailed and thorough), then we valued some of her attributes (eye for details, ability to spot trends), and last, we linked what she did with how it helped the company (helps us know whether or not we should proceed).

Sally leaves the conversation feeling rewarded and recognized, but also clear on how she contributes to something larger, such as the company. This helps her feel valued and heightens her sense of purpose at work. This type of reward and recognition inspires repeat performances.

Instead of linking her report to how it benefits the company we could have easily linked her efforts to how they help you as her manager, or how they help serve the customer. Your choices are many, but the important thing is to link behavior and/or employee attributes with a tangible consequence of those said behaviors. (For more on this, download the recognition codes at www.nineminutesonmonday.com.)

The first key to great reward and recognition is to do it regularly. I once had a manager tell me that he didn't believe he should recognize someone each week. The man had eight direct reports. This means that if he recognized one employee each week, it would be two months before he got back to the first one again. Can you imagine going eight weeks without your boss saying anything positive to you? Unfortunately, many employees can. If you don't recognize any employees during a given week, let it be because you decided not to, not that you simply forgot.

The second key is to practice. Each week during your leadership planning time take one minute to ask the question, "Whom will I reward or recognize this week?" Find at least one employee to whom you can give the Midas touch. The more you practice valuing achievements, attributes, and contributions, the better and more natural you will become at doing it. Rewards and recognition help increase engagement among your staff and contribute to a more positive and motivated workplace. After all, who doesn't want to work in that kind of environment? I know search and rescue dogs do!

MINUTE THREE SUMMARY

Key Lessons
- What is rewarded gets repeated.
- Reward and recognition meet the need to be valued.
- Reward and recognition are powerful tools to help shape behavior.

Key Question
- Whom will I reward or recognize this week?

Key Action Steps
- Go to www.nineminutesonmonday.com and download the recognition codes.
- Use the recognition codes to give someone the Midas touch.

MINUTE 3

Whom will I reward or recognize
this week?

$\left(8 \right)$

The Second Paycheck
The Need for Purpose

I set myself on fire, and people come to watch me burn.

—John Wesley

In December 2009, Nick Harris of Ottawa, Kansas, witnessed a hor-
rific accident. A Mercury sedan, while in reverse, had run over a six-
year-old girl, pinning her under the tire. Nick ran to the scene as fast as
he could, grabbed the rear end of the car, and lifted it off the child. The
six-year-old suffered only a concussion and a few scrapes.

Unable to understand his moment of superhuman strength, five-
foot-seven, 185-pound Harris attempted to lift other cars later that day
and couldn't.

We have all heard stories of superhuman feats in times of emer-
gency. The human body has amazing reserves to go above and beyond
what we would normally believe to be possible. Nick Harris was no
doubt aided by the body's ability to surge chemicals such as epineph-
rine, which prepare it for moments of extreme exertion. Wouldn't it
be nice if we could package this? Imagine an energy drink that not
only boosted alertness but enabled you to lift cars. While we are day-
dreaming, wouldn't it be nice if there was something called superhuman motivation? Imagine if there was a pill that would turn staff
members' motivation into overdrive and increase their productivity by

100 percent. Would you be interested? A psychologist and professor named Adam Grant at the Wharton School of Business may have found what you are looking for.

In 2008, Adam Grant went to a call center of the fundraising department at a university and divided the employees into three groups. A typical day for these folks involved phoning alumni and others in order to solicit donations to be used for scholarships. The first group acted as the control, while the other two were provided with material to read. To the members of the second group was given a pamphlet that outlined the various benefits they were reaping by working this job. It helped them see how they were increasing their phone skills, interpersonal skills, and so on. In essence, it was a WIIFM (What's in it for me?) exercise. In the third group, Mr. Grant simply gave the employees a collection of letters to read that had been written by past scholarship recipients outlining how the scholarships had made a difference to their lives. The first group—the control group—did nothing differently.

Mr. Grant returned a month later to see if either of his interventions had affected the motivation and productivity of the fundraisers. The results were nothing short of amazing. The control group had no increase in the number of pledges or donations over their previous months, which was no surprise. Participants in the second group, the ones who had received the information outlining the benefits of doing the job, also had no significant change. The WIIFM mentality did not seem to affect their overall motivation and productivity. The real shock came from what happened in the third group. Members of this group, who had read the letters from past scholarship recipients, turned out to have *doubled* their pledges and more than *doubled* the amount of money they brought in the previous month.

How does a group of fundraisers who read a few letters from people they do not know end up doubling productivity in a single month? It sounds like superhuman motivation to me. The answer lies in what I call the second paycheck.

THE SECOND PAYCHECK

I had an opportunity to work with a not-for-profit organization that was involved in the field of family services. These people do fantastic work serving their communities, running programs, and providing support so that families can function and thrive. Like many not-for-profits, it was limited by how much money it could pay its staff. This resulted in a high turnover rate among new hires. Regardless of how much members of the organization warned new hires of the low pay, they still seemed to lose a lot of them after the first paycheck. I was asked this question: "How can we keep our new hires when so many seem to quit after they receive their first paycheck?"

"The solution," I said, "is that you have to start giving out the second paycheck before you hand out the first."

The *second paycheck* is that moment of connection between purpose and pay. It is the moment when we tap into that wonderful motivator called purpose. *Purpose* is our "why" and is fueled by an inner source of intrinsic motivation that derives its reward from the job itself. Connecting purpose to pay is essential in motivating today's employees, especially when we are unable to pay higher salaries or compete with the luxurious benefit packages some organizations are able to offer their employees.

I advised them to take the new hires and get them involved in purposeful work within the first two weeks. Instead of placing them in the office, the members of the organization needed to allow them to interact with some of the clients. For example, they could take the new hires on house calls where they were providing some support services or training for parents. Then, on the way back to the office, give them the second paycheck. For this family services organization it might be a simple conversation that goes something like this:

"Do you realize what we just did for this family? That seven-year-old boy is going to come home from school today, and his parents will not be fighting. They are also going to start carving out some special one-on-one time just to be with him. We definitely impacted that little boy's life today."

This is the second paycheck, and it is priceless.

If the family services organization could do that a couple of times with their new hires before their first paycheck arrives, then the amount of the check would become secondary because, at the end of the day, people seek significance before they seek financial reward.

The second paycheck is powerful, but how do you practically connect purpose to pay? Here are three questions to help you achieve that connection and increase your employee's intrinsic motivation.

Whom Do We Serve?

Employees often have a limited view of whom they serve. Too many people fail to see beyond the walls of their company when asked the question, whom do you work for?

If we return to the study done by Adam Grant, we see this principle in action. How did the members of the third group of fundraisers double their effectiveness from the previous month? Did they make more calls? On the calls they did make, were they more passionate, convincing, or sincere? Research that is more detailed would be needed to know exactly what they did differently, but the power is not in the techniques; it lies in the motivation. They were fueled by purpose. While employees were reading letters from past scholarship participants, a picture is able to emerge of whom it is that they are serving. Although their paycheck is made out to them by the university, a far more compelling and motivating employer is able to manifest itself. The fundraisers are able to experience a shift in motivation as they begin to see that they really work for all the people who are unable to afford the opportunity to attend this prestigious institution.

Serving people is always more motivating than working for a company. If you can help your employees see who it is that they serve, whether it's a customer, a coworker, a segment of society, or a cause, it ignites something inside them. This fire elevates their commitment, resulting in improved performance.

What Job Has Our Product or Service Been Hired to Do?

Laurie was a cosmetics and day spa owner who ran an impressive business. Over the years she had built a progressively strong company and was a leader in her industry. Laurie was incredibly organized and had a detailed system in place in order to help her employees sell products. She was very friendly with all the women on her staff and believed in people to a fault. Overall, Laurie was a great boss. But she was having a problem with some of her employees; they seemed to lack motivation. She felt as if some of the women were not trying hard enough to push sales or to go for the up-sell, despite her thorough training in this area.

Part of the problem was in how employees saw their jobs. In their minds, they sold cosmetics and day spa services. I told Laurie and her managers that cosmetics are just a product that is hired to do a job. I asked them, "So what job do you think cosmetics are hired to do? In other words, why do you think women buy makeup?" To which they answered, "To feel more beautiful."

Many companies sell a product or service. The truth is that your customers do not really want your product; they are actually looking for a result that your product or service provides. Therefore, your product is simply hired to do a job, and in Laurie's case it was to help women feel beautiful.

This may seem like an exercise in semantics, but which do you think is more motivating? "We sell cosmetics, and we are trying to sell X amount of product this month." Or, "We help women feel beautiful."

And so began the mind shift in motivation. Over the coming weeks I began to work with some of her managers to help them approach motivation from a different angle. Selling makeup is a lot different from thinking, "I help women feel beautiful." One day a woman came in for a makeover. After her transformation, she made a comment to one of the staff members.

"I feel so confident," she said as she beamed.

I advised Laurie to take that sound bite and pass it on to the entire staff at the next team meeting as further evidence of what job their products are hired to do. This may seem subtle, but when a makeup artist approaches a client with the intent to help her feel beautiful and confident, then when it comes time to suggest other products, it is no longer an awkward sales pitch. The makeup artists do not have to stress about the transition from painting faces to suggesting other products in order to increase their sales numbers. Because their motivation comes from a different place—one grounded in purpose—a more intrinsic and thus more powerful motivation kicks in.

How Do You Make a Difference Here?

One final question to help you link purpose to pay is helping employees see how their role makes a difference—to you, the team, or the company. This is one of the reasons why employees need to see a clear connection between what they do and how it impacts the success of the company. I have worked with some large companies where some employees do not know how the company makes money. It is tough in that kind of environment to link purpose to pay. Your staff needs to see how their daily efforts contribute to the larger picture of the organization. It goes beyond the company. Purpose can be found through helping employees see how they make a difference to the team and to you, their boss. Helping employees understand how their own pursuit of excellence mitigates some of the stress experienced by their peers will not only improve the team overall but will contribute to their sense of their own importance to the organization.

THE POWER OF STORY

A picture is worth a thousand words, maybe even ten thousand. Recently I was conducting a day-long training session with a company and its managers. The company was in the business of waste management and recycling. I guided the managers through an exercise to help them link purpose to pay. After working for a few minutes in groups, I had them report different ways that they might connect purpose to pay. People began by saying things like, "We help the environment," and, "We provide clean drinking water for the community."

While these were true, they were lacking the emotional connection necessary to arouse purpose. One of the reasons purpose is such a powerful motivator is that it invokes emotion. Emotion is like the nitrous oxide button on a race car that, once pushed, results in an explosion of power. Emotion, however, is not aroused by generic statements such as, "We help the environment," but, rather, by stories and word pictures.

As humans, we have communicated for thousands of years via story. Stories are important because they help us form images in our brain, and, for whatever reason, pictures are easier to hold onto than pure data. I still remember my physics teacher asking us to figure out whether the bullet we fired from 100 yards away would hit the monkey who simultaneously jumped out of the tree. To this day I can't recall the formulas for figuring out the problem, but I can still picture the poor monkey jumping out of the tree while my bullet sped his way.

Working with the group of recycling managers I asked, "How do you help the environment?"

A woman at the back answered, "Well, we recycle paper so we save trees!"

Saving trees is good but still too generic.

"How many trees?" I asked.

There was silence because no one knew. Someone did, however, have a record of the amount of paper they recycled each month and knew how many tons of paper equaled one tree. Before long, someone else crunched the numbers and soon we had the answer.

"We recycle, on average, 1,446 trees a month."

You could feel a sense of pride come over the room because, for the first time, this organization realized that every month it saves 1,446 trees. Isn't that much more visually effective than the statement "We help the environment"?

Let's revisit the Adam Grant experiment at the university call center. Imagine if, instead of letters, Adam Grant had given the third group a list of purpose statements such as: "You help people get into college who normally could not afford it, and that helps open doors for them that will change their lives."

While statements such as these are true, would they result in a doubling of money raised? I doubt it, because although they do help link purpose to pay, they would fail to engage the emotions the way the personal letters did. It's one thing to say that you help people get into college; it's quite another when those same people paint a picture for you of how it changed their lives.

Word pictures and stories are powerful tools for communicating. It is what humans have relied on for thousands of years to pass along the wisdom of the ages. Stories have a way of making information stick, partly because they are visual, and partly because they invoke emotion. I remember reading about a farmer trying to explain the differences between organic farming and his previous methods of using pesticides and chemicals. His presentation was filled with evidence, statistics, and reasons, but not a lot of it was connecting. It wasn't until the farmer changed his approach and said, "Look, before I switched to organic farming, when I would come in from the field and my kids would run out to hug me, I had to say, 'Stop, you can't touch me right now. You have to wait until I have changed my clothes.' Now that I have switched to organic farming, when I come in from the fields, if my kids want to run and give me hug, they are free to do so." With this imagery the audience "got it." Even to this day, I still think of that story when I am in the grocery store.

Stories and images help make a message stick. When it comes to the second paycheck, the more specific you can be, the better. It is one thing for your employee Mary to know that her position as a loan officer for small business start-ups helps the company secure capital. It's quite another when she sees how she helped an entrepreneur launch his dream.

Connecting purpose to pay helps meet your employee's need for significance. Giving the second paycheck does not have to be complicated. Nor do you have to search for the perfect image or words to say. The main idea is to help your staff members connect to the bigger picture of whom they serve, what job they really do, and how they make a difference. Just like that superhuman strength that helped Nick Harris lift a car off a little girl, you will be amazed at how the second paycheck can arouse a deep-seated motivation among your staff members, springing from a deep desire to make a difference in the lives of those around them.

MINUTE FOUR SUMMARY

Key Lessons

- People have a need to feel significant.
- Connecting purpose to pay is one of the most powerful motivators in the world.
- Find purpose by asking three questions:
  1. Whom do we serve?
  2. What job has our product or service been hired to do?
  3. How do you make a difference here?
- Stories and images help arouse emotion and purpose.

Key Question

- Whom will I give the second paycheck to this week?

Key Action Steps

- Go to www.nineminutesonmonday.com and download the connecting purpose to pay exercise.
- Connect purpose to pay for one employee this week.

· MINUTE FOUR ·

*Whom will I give the second
paycheck to this week?*

PART III

Secondary Needs and Implementation

$\left(\begin{array}{c}9\end{array}\right)$

Control
The Need for Autonomy

> *Those who deny freedom to others deserve it not for themselves.*
>
> —Abraham Lincoln

"Free at last. Free at last. Thank God Almighty, we are free at last!" When Martin Luther King spoke these words from the steps of the Lincoln Memorial, they ignited the hearts of millions of listeners. At the core of his message was a dream of freedom and equality. It resonated with people because at the heart of every human is an innate desire to be free. When we are free, we have what is called autonomy. Autonomy is our desire to be self-directed, and it is very motivating.

While autonomy is a powerful source of motivation, it often takes a back seat to carrots and sticks. The stick is used to threaten people and push them toward something, while the carrot's job is to entice and pull them toward a reward. Both of these are used extensively in business today. Frederick Herzberg, an American psychologist and one of the most influential names in business management, referred to these as KITA motivators (short for kick in the you-know-what). Carrots and sticks are also known as extrinsic motivators because the motivation originates from outside of you (e.g., your angry boss). Carrots and sticks are everywhere. You submit your work to your boss because she gives you a deadline, you stay late to finish the project because you will get a bonus, and you study for your exam because you are going to be tested. Carrots and sticks are so woven into our culture that we barely recognize them for what they are—external stimuli moving us to action in order to receive a reward or avoid some form of punishment. They run on a simple "if-then" formula. "*If* I do this, *then* I will get that."

While carrots and stick certainly do motivate people, they have some serious flaws. The problem with if-then types of rewards and punishments is that they are not self-sustaining. If you remove the reward, or the punishment, the desired behavior stops, or at the very least is significantly reduced. This places an enormous burden on managers to be continually providing a steady diet of fresh carrots and/or bigger sticks in order to keep their employees motivated. This is one of the most taxing activities for many managers. Extrinsic motivation is not only shortsighted, but it also does not bring out the best in employees.

At the other side of the spectrum is a far more powerful source of motivation, called intrinsic motivation. *Intrinsic motivation* comes from within. Instead of carrots and sticks, think energy drinks. Intrinsic motivation is the reason why you volunteer at your church or local food hamper, and why you would drive all the way across town because a friend of yours was sick. After they say, "Thank you," you respond, "No worries. It was my pleasure." And, it *was* your pleasure because that is what intrinsic motivation is about. The reward comes from the good feelings of doing the task itself. Intrinsic motivation is what pulls you to act on your own volition regardless of what anyone else may be doing to push or pull you in a certain direction.

The differences between these two types of motivation do not stop here. A growing body of research shows that when people are intrinsically motivated, they will work harder, persist longer, be more creative, use more flexible thinking in problem solving, and use more conceptual learning strategies when trying to master new material. And intrinsic motivation will also contribute to higher overall well-being. In fact, study after study has shown that trying to motivate people with external rewards or punishments only reduces their capacity to perform optimally. The only time this is not true is when the job at hand requires little to no thought, that is, simple A + B = C type of work. However, as soon as you require even elementary cognitive thought processes to accomplish a task, if-then types of rewards actually diminish performance. If high performers are what you seek, then you definitely need to leverage the power of intrinsic motivation in your workplace. But why is there such a massive difference between intrinsic and extrinsic motivation? The answer lies in our need for autonomy.

OUR NEED TO BE IN CONTROL

In 1969 a young doctoral student in psychology named Edward Deci at Carnegie-Mellon University in Pittsburgh conducted an experiment to test the effects that rewards would have on intrinsic motivation. The experiment called for two groups to solve the then-popular Soma puzzles. The Soma puzzle was a game released by Parker Brothers consisting of six wooden blocks that had to be put together in the correct sequence in order to make a perfect cube. In addition, the blocks could also be stacked together to create shapes such as dogs, couches, and airplanes. The puzzle provided its own source of intrinsic motivation by challenging one's creativity and rewarding people with a sense of achievement for each shape they created. After dividing into two groups, one group (Group A) was given an extrinsic motivator by offering them a small amount of money for each puzzle they solved, while the other group (Group B) was offered no such reward. Edward Deci wanted to answer the question, what will happen to the level of intrinsic motivation in Group A, which was being paid (an extrinsic motivator) compared with Group B, which was not?

After the students played with the puzzles for about half an hour, they were told that the research was over and that the experimenter had to leave the room momentarily in order to enter some data into a computer. While the experimenter was gone, the students were free to do as they pleased. On the table next to them were various magazines they could look through if they pleased. The real experiment, however, was just beginning. It was during this time that experimenters secretly observed the students to see what they would do with their free time. Would the students who had been paid to play continue to work on the puzzles or would they stop? As it turned out, students who were paid to solve the puzzles were far less likely to continue playing with the puzzles than those who had been doing it "for fun" all along.

By introducing a monetary reward, researchers had stolen the more effective intrinsic motivation from the students. Why would a monetary reward affect the source of a person's motivation? The reason for this shift is related to our perception of control. One of our biggest psychological needs is our need for autonomy. We want to feel that we direct and have control over our lives. When anyone tries to exert control over us, there is a part of us that seems to rebel. My wife helps people lose weight and knows that motivation is important. When people's motivation to trim down is external, such as a nagging spouse or public pressure, they will rarely experience long-term success. Such external motivators often lead to a sort of inward revolt, resulting in a conspiracy of self-sabotage. One of her clients who had the nagging husband confessed to my wife that whenever she was angry with him, she would sneak off to the convenience store and eat junk food. Her actions were a mini-rebellion against the external control her husband was trying to subject her to.

Because we live in a largely carrot and stick world, the concept of autonomy can seem hard to grasp. The fact remains, however, that the most powerful self-sustaining source of motivation is that which comes from within. The good news is that you as a manager can do several things to help your employees enjoy a greater sense of freedom and control at work which will increase their level of motivation.

RELEASE THE PRISONERS

If you were attending Stanford University during the early 1970s, you may have come across an advertisement asking students to participate in a paid, two-week-long study. It was the brainchild of Philip Zimbardo, a psychology professor at Stanford. Zimbardo turned the basement of one of the buildings at the university into a mock prison. Twenty-four students were selected, half to serve as guards and half as prisoners. The experiment was to last two weeks but had to be terminated after only six days because the student guards became increasingly aggressive, and the student prisoners showed signs of extreme stress, resignation, and depression.

Although there are many lessons that have been drawn from this famous study, one interesting point relates to our discussion here. It has to do with people's perception of control.

The student prisoners entered into the experiment of their own free will. Even though they would be paid a small amount for participating, they were told that they could quit at any time they wanted. But something happened when, through a series of misunderstandings, the students began to believe that they actually had no choice and that they really *were* prisoners. As their role shifted from that of a volunteer to one of an actual prisoner (at least in their own minds), negative emotions such as depression and extreme signs of stress began to manifest themselves.

Our perception of how much control we have exerts an incredible impact on our motivation, happiness, and overall well-being. Patients who have control over administering their own morphine report less pain than those who receive the same amount automatically. Employees who enjoy a sense of autonomy at work take fewer sick days than those who don't. One of the reasons is that autonomy is a buffer to stress. When we feel in control, we are more proactive when dealing with challenges and stressors. When we are subject to a challenging environment that we have little or no control over (can you say "micro-management"?), we can actually learn to become helpless.

Martin Seligman, in a series of experiments, discovered that when animals and humans are exposed to painful situations over which they have no control, they eventually give up trying to escape. When they are later subjected to a new, similar situation where there *is* an opportunity to escape the pain, most will not even attempt to try. They have learned to be helpless. This learned helplessness creates motivational, cognitive, and emotional deficits. Motivational in that subjects no longer try, cognitive in that their learning is impaired, and emotional by experiencing signs and symptoms of depression. Employees can experience a similar type of learned helplessness after repeated failed attempts to influence their work environment. Employees will eventually give up trying to have an influence and resign themselves to the status quo. This might make a micro-managing boss happy, but it's hardly what brings out the best in people.

When employees work in environments where they have little to no control, they can feel a bit like the volunteer prisoners in Zimbardo's Stanford experiment. This kind of environment practically kills initiation among workers. This is also the reason why no one wants to work for a micromanaging boss. People need *some* autonomy, and it does not always have to manifest itself in large ways like flexible work schedules. Some of the easiest ways to increase an employee's feeling of autonomy are simple and within your control.

Give Choices When Possible
After recently relocating to a new city, my wife asked me what I thought.

"It's nice," I told her.

Unconvinced, she said, "But ...?"

"Well, I just wish there was a professional hockey team here. I can't go to any games," I confessed.

"But you never went to any games in our old city," she remarked.

"I know, but I *could* have gone to a game if I wanted to," I said.

I was suffering from a minor loss of one of the choices I had enjoyed in my previous home.

Choice and autonomy go hand in hand. If you want to foster employees' autonomy, then find ways to give them a greater degree of choice or flexibility in how they carry out their role. While this may be impossible in some jobs, for most roles there are a surprising number of options. Every mountain may have only one summit and there are usually time parameters that must be adhered to, but beyond that the choices of which routes to take to the top are limitless. Giving people a chance to think on their own and providing them with as much choice as the limits will allow will increase their intrinsic motivation. It is easy to believe that we know the best way to do the job, but that doesn't mean it is the best way for our employees to do the job. Try to find even small ways to give your employees some choice in how they do their job.

When choice is not an option, try to provide a rationale for why they need to perform a certain task a certain way. A person who hears why is more likely to internalize and voluntarily accept the externally imposed restrictions. Once internalized, people exert more voluntary effort, even in uninteresting activities.

Give Them Input

Two teams were assigned to create two separate wall murals in order to spice up a run-down neighborhood. One group of team members was given the image they were to paint, while the other team was asked for input and ideas. Even though a final decision was made by the artist in charge, everyone had a chance to contribute. Which team do you think put more heart into the mural?

When employees are asked for input, it not only makes them feel respected and important, but it gives them a chance to affect their work environment. This perception has a significant influence on their sense of control and autonomy. After all, how many prisoners are asked for input? This can be difficult for those managers who are naturally controlling by nature, and many of us are more controlling than we realize. Remember, not everything has to be done your way; when you open yourself up to this possibility, it gives your staff an opportunity to provide input. An added benefit of seeking input from your staff is that you pool the collective wisdom of your team. You never know where the next great idea may come from. One caution on input, however: if you seek input but never implement anything anyone says, then you will send your staff a message that although you are asking, you are not really listening. I saw this once with a manager I was coaching who told me she no longer offers any of her ideas. Even though the company had asked for input, it never implemented any of the ideas. She figured why bother anymore.

Put Them in Charge

Frederick Herzberg, when identifying workplace motivators, found that employees listed "increasing responsibility" as one of their top workplace satisfiers. When employees are able to take on more responsibility, it usually comes with more choice and input into how things are done. This is one of the reasons why those in management are typically more engaged than the average frontline employee; managers usually enjoy the choice and extra input that comes with their increased responsibility. Increased responsibility and promotions are also forms of feedback that tell employees they are growing and contributing and that they are valuable to the organization.

While you may not be able to promote each of your employees, you can still find creative ways to help them take on greater levels of responsibility. One idea is to encourage each staff member to become a specialized expert in a certain area. This helps employees feel an increase in importance and ownership of a certain topic or skill. By becoming the go-to person in a particular area, employees attach a certain amount of personal pride with the title. This personal investment fuels engagement and adds more purpose to their work. Purpose, as we have already discussed, is a huge source of employee engagement.

Whether you are building puzzles or assembling jumbo jets, carrots and sticks will get you only so far. When employees feel a sense of control over their work, it helps meet their need for autonomy. Autonomy is important because it is one of the main sources of intrinsic motivation. When people are motivated from the inside, they invest more of their heart and effort into their work. By providing your staff with such things as flexibility, input, choice, and increased responsibility, you will enrich their workplace and their lives. After all, don't you enjoy a little freedom too? In your nine-minute planning time think of one simple thing you can do this week to increase autonomy for one of your staff members.

MINUTE FIVE SUMMARY

Key Lessons

- When employees experience autonomy, it increases their level of self-motivation.
- Self-motivation or intrinsic motivation leads to increased effort, creativity, engagement, conceptual thinking, and overall well-being.

Key Question

- How can I promote the feeling of autonomy in one employee this week?

Action Steps

- Seek someone's input.
- Give someone choice.
- Put someone in charge.

How can I promote a feeling of autonomy in one employee this week?

(10)

Foam Pits and Trampolines
The Need to Grow

> *The idea is to improve the man, not to reach the top of mountains. Climbing only makes sense if you consider the man.*
>
> —Walter Bonatti

"Don't worry about it." At least that's what Lt. Kermit Tyler told the radar operators who had picked up an unusually large mass on his screen heading toward Oahu. It was shortly after seven o'clock in the morning on December 7, 1941, that Lt. Kermit Tyler, a U.S. Army fighter pilot, received the phone call from a nearby radar station. It was Lt. Tyler's second day on the job at the tracking center, and he had little understanding of radar. The one young serviceman who originally spotted the planes was still getting used to his *first* day on the job. Mistaking the mass on the screen to be a fleet of B-17 bombers that were due in later that day, Lt. Tyler told the two men not to worry about it. Unfortunately, the dots on the radar were not B-17 bombers but, rather, Japanese planes racing toward Pearl Harbor for a surprise attack, which would plunge the United States into World War II. Later, after an investigation, Lt. Tyler was cleared of any negligence on his part because he, along with the two other radar operators, had not been adequately trained.

Last year my wife and I decided to try something new. We signed up for adult gymnastics. Despite a little ribbing from my pub buddies, my wife and I showed up on the first night ready to expand our horizons. We arrived at an old brick building located on the outskirts of downtown. This gymnastics gym was like a big play place for adults, minus the fries and happy meals. There were bars, pulleys, ropes, trampolines, and every color of mat you could imagine. The most inviting piece of equipment was the yawning foam pit waiting to swallow you up in the corner of the room. After warming up with the group, Sean, one of the gymnasts, spent some time with my wife and me teaching us how to do back flips on the trampoline. That night after the session, we drove home, giddy with how much fun we'd had. It was different, it was challenging, and it introduced us to a whole new world of challenges in which we could grow.

As we get older, it is easy to fall into the rut of a routine life. Days become predictable, and that's a good thing because most of our energy is needed to survive the workweek. But this is not an inspiring road, and despite the security and predictability our routines may offer us, we were meant for more. Deep within every human being is the need to grow.

STAFF DEVELOPMENT

One recent worldwide study on the workplace revealed that "the opportunity to grow and develop" was the second highest driver of employee engagement. Your staff members want to grow, and if they do not find opportunities within your organization to do so, they will be tempted to look somewhere else. Vast numbers of employees still feel like they are not being developed. Such gaps largely exist because most managers are too busy to think about the ongoing development of their people. Yet if we want out employees to engage their talents, we must help them meet their need for growth. To do this, we must first understand what role we play in the growth process.

In larger companies, many managers defer training to the corporate trainer or employee development department. Others wait for human resources to initiate some type of training program. In smaller companies, managers are usually so busy wearing multiple hats that staff training rarely makes it to their schedule. While there will always be a variety of great seminars, courses, and other tools to equip your staff, there is nothing quite like the ongoing training managers can provide for their direct reports. More than anyone else in your organization, you carry the greatest potential to affect the growth and development of your people. This is partly the result of the weighted relationships we discussed in Chapter 3, but also the trust generated while working alongside your direct report week in and week out. In order to help your employees grow without it costing you a lot of time or money, there are four steps that will simplify your staff development. They are clarity, challenge, support, and feedback.

Clarity

One of the challenges of training staff members is that we often do not know where to begin. Sometimes our thinking is limited to training methods such as seminars and courses when, in fact, a plethora of other methods are available. *How* the training is administered is not as important as *what* training is administered. Helping your people grow begins first with clarity. It is hard to help someone develop if you're not sure where they actually need to develop. A good question to ask yourself regarding your employees is, "Where do they need to grow in order for them to be more effective than they are now?" While some employees have a clear picture for themselves, many rely on their manager to direct them. When I asked one senior manager whom I was coaching what area he most wanted to grow in, he told me he wasn't sure. So then I asked him what area his boss thinks he needs to grow in, and he responded, "I'm not sure, he's never told me." This senior manager was caught in a rut with no clear idea on where he needed to grow.

When it comes to growth, there is no one size fits all. Different jobs require different competencies, and failing to recognize this will result in bland, unfocused training. When you're trying to outline clear areas for growth, it sometimes helps to break needs down into four broad areas: knowledge, technical skills, career skills, and behaviors/attitudes. Separating growth needs into these areas makes it easier to zero in on specific topics.

1. *Knowledge.* Every job requires some degree of acquired knowledge. Sometimes we do not equate acquisition of knowledge with growth, but the two are closely related. I coached one manager who decided to make it his miniproject to learn the ins and outs of one of his company's energy plants. He was responsible for giving the office updates regarding the plant but, other than a basic knowledge of the operations, he did not know much else about it. His decision to know the plant in detail provided him with an opportunity to grow, which not only benefited him but the entire organization. Another manager I was coaching felt as if no one respected her at the senior management weekly meetings. She decided to become more knowledgeable about her industry by reading trade journals and networking so she could bring more value to the Monday morning meeting. Over time she was able to contribute more and feel more confident among the other senior managers. Knowledge is power.

2. *Technical skills.* Any technical skill that employees need in order to do their job, whether it's a computer program, a work process, or simply how to drive a forklift, is essential. Training in technical skills is probably the easiest to identify and deploy.

3. *Career skills.* Career skills make up a very broad category and are unique to each job. For example, someone in management must learn how to resolve conflict, how to motivate, how to lead a meeting effectively, and how to deal with poor performers, just to name

a few. Someone in sales must learn an equally large number of career skills. The key question to ask is, "What skills are going to help make this employee more effective in his current role or get him ready for the next level of responsibility?"

4. *Behaviors and attitudes.* Your job as a manager is to promote effective behaviors that are going to lead to some desirable result. Behaviors and attitudes are prime areas for training and growth, but first they must be identified. Once they are crystal clear, you are able to help correct any ineffective behaviors and attitudes as they appear. For example, a sales rep may need to learn to be more aggressive, or a young manager may need to control his facial expressions upon hearing bad news. The key is to begin to identify which behaviors and attitudes your direct reports need to develop in order to be successful in their roles.

Once you have identified several areas for possible growth, you can then decide on the best way to deploy the training. Regardless of the methods, growth is a process, and although it begins with clarity, it usually includes some type of stretching of employees outside their comfort zone. Sometimes during management training sessions I will ask people to write down the names of three people who have helped them perform at their best. Beside each name I ask them to write down what it was that the person did to have this effect on them. The answers are usually the same no matter where I go. Managers tell me it was someone who challenged them, and someone who supported and believed in them. It may not be obvious at first glance, but both of these are essential parts of the growth cycle and are within your direct circle of influence.

Challenge

Very little growth takes place inside someone's comfort zone. Growth requires stretching and trying new things. Most people will not initiate this process on their own. Just as a mother bird eventually nudges her young out of the nest, leaders must periodically nudge their direct reports a few feet beyond where they feel comfortable in order to initiate the growth process. People will naturally respond with moans, complaints, and various facial expressions that communicate their reluctance. Most of this is masked fear. The greatest disservice you can do to your employees is to never challenge them. When you ask Jill to lead the team meeting in two weeks, she may try to back out simply because she's afraid. But if she needs to learn how to lead meetings, then this is a great challenge for her to take on. It certainly will push her outside her comfort zone.

How far out of their comfort zone you push employees is the key. Too far and you will push them beyond their own belief of what is possible, resulting in decreased engagement. If it's not far enough, they won't feel the challenge that motivates them to double up their efforts. To be on the safe side, start small in order to create small wins that boost confidence. As you learn more about staff members, you can then progressively challenge them to get farther and farther outside their comfort zone. Take some time to consider how you might provide a gentle nudge to each of your direct reports to push him or her into a place of growth.

Support and Believe in Them

Venturing beyond our comfort zones typically places us in a position of lowered confidence. Out there, it's always helpful to have an extra dose of support. If you recall from Csíkszentmihályi's work on flow, optimal performance is found when there is a balance between the level of challenge and the perception of one's skill to handle the challenge. As a manager, you want to help your direct reports have confidence in their ability to handle the challenge you have assigned them. Boosting someone's feelings of competence is an integral part of a manager's job. Albert Bandura's research on self-efficacy (our belief in our own competence) has found that there are multiple ways to boost the competence of your staff.

1. *Modeling.* When employees observe someone else doing the task, it increases their own confidence to attempt it themselves. Modeling is even more powerful when the person they are observing is close to them in either age or position.

2. *Past experience.* Success breeds success. When employees are reminded of past situations they have overcome that are similar to their present challenge, it increases their feelings of self-efficacy. In fact, past performance is the most powerful source of increased competence. Sometimes, especially when they're afraid, people tend to forget what they have accomplished in the past. A simple reminder can do wonders for their confidence and desire to commit.

3. *Pep talks.* Words of comfort and reassurance have a way of calming people down and refocusing them on the task at hand. Pep talks are an easy way for managers to engage employees during times of stretching. Even the simple act of believing in someone has a powerful effect on their behavior. Employees who might doubt their own abilities are able to borrow some of your faith, just until they get back their own.

One day I was driving my teenage daughter to a dance audition. She was understandably nervous because we had just moved to a new city, and she did not know anybody. Going into a dance audition while feeling overly nervous is not going to help you perform at your peak. So on the ride there, I reminded her of the past auditions in which she had performed well, and I continued to give her a bit of a pep talk regarding her skill level. I was trying to boost her confidence. When I had finished, she said, "Thanks. That really helps." It was one of those moments when you think, "Oh, maybe my teenager *does* listen to me!"

Employees may not enjoy being pushed outside their comfort zone, and it's not something you can do every day. But, once they take on the challenge and experience success, they will look to you with gratitude for believing in them even when they did not believe in themselves. This creates a powerful bond between an employee and a manager.

Feedback—Did I Grow?

In our house, on the wall close to the refrigerator, you will find a mess of pencil lines and dates. It has somehow become the Robbins family growth chart. My kids regularly stand against the wall and, while trying to hold the pencil level above their head, they make a small tick mark. The amusing part to this ritual was that when our kids were younger, they would sometimes check themselves within days of their last measurement, just to see if they had grown.

Because growth is often hard for us to see ourselves, we rely on outside information to confirm that we have indeed made progress. This feedback is important because growth, like beauty, is in the eye of the beholder. If one of your employees is growing but does not realize it, then in her mind she is not growing at all. We have talked about the power of feedback several times already, and here, again, is another example of where it needs to be applied. It is imperative that in addition to helping your employees grow, you let them know when you see progress. This feedback helps them stay motivated, increases their confidence, and continues the forward momentum that was begun earlier.

THE BEST WAY TO DEVELOP YOUR PEOPLE

While sending your employees off to seminars and courses will be an integral part of their development, nothing beats the day-in and day-out coaching and mentoring by you, the boss. Most employees do not enjoy the experience of ongoing development, because their manager is not sure how to do it or because the manager is just too busy and has not established it as part of a routine.

Coaching your employees does not have to be complicated as some would have you believe, nor does it take hours of your time in face-to-face sessions. Great coaching is quick, on the fly, and practical.

When my wife and I joined the gymnastics class, we needed help. You cannot learn a back handspring from reading a book or by attending a lecture, especially when you are in your forties. What you need is a coach. In our class there were between 15 and 20 adults, but only one head coach. Each night after a brief warm-up, we were turned loose to play on any apparatus of our choice. One of my favorites was the long trampoline. Imagine a trampoline 30 feet long and 5 feet wide with a deep foam pit at one end. If you dove into the pit you would disappear beneath a sea of square foam cubes. That was a lot of fun. The long trampoline is mainly used to practice tumbling. I desperately wanted to learn how to do a handspring and, after watching a few others, I began taking my turn. Gymnastics is a very technical sport. There is much to learn in order to pull off some of the moves. While having a one-on-one private coach would have been ideal, I was able to have the next best thing. Sean coached all of us. You might wonder how one coach could possibly assist 15 to 20 different people during a two-hour period while we all worked on different pieces of equipment.

Sean made his way around the gym. When he came to the long trampoline, he watched me attempt a front handspring, which almost always ended with me on my back looking up at the ceiling. Sean quickly pulled me aside and said something like, "Okay, great. You had good speed, but next time I want you to reach farther with your arms before you plant them," stretching out his arms to demonstrate. "Now let's try it again."

Under his watchful eye, I attempted it again, this time focusing on extending my reach. After landing on my butt, which was an improvement from my back, Sean said, "Okay, better. Now I want you to keep practicing that tonight."

Then, as quickly as he had appeared, Sean was off to the uneven bars to help someone with a dismount while I spent the next few minutes focused on improving my handspring. During the night Sean might make his way back to me two or three times, and each time his small pieces of advice would help me improve.

Sean and thousands of others like him are evidence that coaching does not have to be a long and arduous process. He made good use of his time, and I felt as though I was growing, so I kept coming back week after week.

What made Sean such an effective coach? The first and most obvious reason was his experience, which taught him what to look for. Knowing what to look for is the starting point when you want to begin developing your employees. When it comes to coaching, you should have a list in mind of which behaviors and skills each of your direct reports need to improve in order to be more effective in his or her role. Each week try to help one of them improve in one small area. Growth is a process. Just as Sean did not try to teach me everything in one night, he knew the progression of learning a front handspring, and he focused me on experiencing success at the next step. When you are able to define these small steps and then coach your employees to experience success, it provides them with small achievements and minimilestones.

I'll never forget, after weeks of practice, when suddenly it clicked, and I could do a front handspring. I felt proud of the accomplishment and grateful to Sean for his help. How much actual one-on-one time did Sean spend with me? Not a lot, but it was laser-focused on getting me to the next step.

The Role of Autonomy in Development

One thing I loved about the gymnastics gym was the choices it offered. As soon as we were finished with the warm-up we were allowed to work in whatever area we wanted. It was motivating to have so much choice. When employees have a say in their development, it increases their buy-in and motivation to improve. In addition to knowing where your employees need to grow, it is important for you to learn where they desire to develop themselves. Employees will usually come up with a list much like the one you created, and this is important because there will be greater commitment to growth if it aligns with an area they desire to improve. Also, asking your direct reports where they want to grow next will sometimes reveal areas that you had not previously thought of, areas that can increase their skill set and help them to be more effective.

Leverage Strengths

There has been a lot of talk in recent years about strength-based management. Helping your employees apply—and grow in—their areas of strength is powerful. When employees are able to tap into their strengths in the workplace, they will feel more confident, more valuable to the team, and, as we learned from flow, more willing to take on more challenging assignments. Employees can often experience the greatest amount of growth in the areas of their natural strengths as opposed to working on improving their weaknesses. Challenging them to take one of their strengths to the next level is a surefire way to motivate their development. Of course, this also requires that you have a good understanding of what strengths they bring to the table. If you have not done so, make a list of strengths and skills that each of your direct reports already possesses. If you are unsure, then ask. This list will be invaluable to you when it comes time to initiate a growth spurt for each of your employees.

Developing your employees not only drives engagement, but it also gives you a host of other areas in which to encourage and motivate your staff. Training and developing can help employees experience mastery and achievement as they embrace a challenge with a goal in mind. It also provides you with an opportunity to reward and recognize their efforts as well as an opening for them to experience some autonomy regarding their career. The biggest error that managers make is trying to complicate the training process. You don't need large initiatives or expensive and time-consuming training sessions. Quick, focused, on-the-fly training can be used to help your staff members meet their need for growth. During your nine-minute planning time, simply think of one employee you can help grow this week and then make it happen.

MINUTE SIX SUMMARY

Key Lessons

- Employees need to grow. It inspires them to engage.
- Growth is a process that involves:
  1. Clarity
  2. Challenge
  3. Support
  4. Feedback
- Coaching on the fly is an excellent way to train your people.

Key Question

- How can I help someone grow this week?

Key Action Item

- Go to www.nineminutesonmonday.com and download the worksheet "grow" in the resource section.

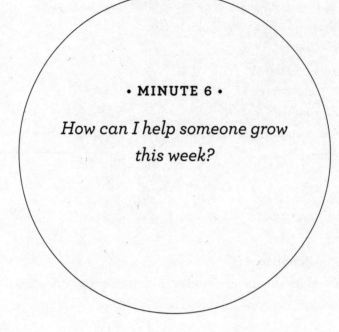

• MINUTE 6 •

*How can I help someone grow
this week?*

(11)

Sticky
The Need to Connect

A single arrow is easily broken, but not ten in a bundle.

—Japanese proverb

In 1914 Ernest Shackleton faced one of the greatest leadership challenges in the history of humanity. Shakleton was an explorer whose quest to become the first person to traverse Antarctica ended in a life-and-death struggle for 27 of his men. While sailing their ship *Endurance* toward the continent of Antarctica, they became locked in pack ice. For months their ship was trapped in a frozen wasteland, unable to move. Gradually, the pressure of the ice began squeezing the ship until it finally cracked and split apart, sinking to the bottom of the Antarctic Ocean. Shackleton and his crew of 27 abandoned the ship, which left them stranded on a giant ice floe with no hope of rescue. Imagine camping on a massive iceberg with no way to communicate with the outside world.

These men had to endure months of freezing temperatures, food rations, and the daily stress of knowing that their lives were at stake. At any moment the ice floe on which they lived could break up, plunging them to a certain icy death. These are ideal conditions for anarchy. Among the many dangers the men faced, Shackleton knew none was more serious than the possibility of a fracture in team morale. He knew of other expeditions in which men had been driven mad by their situation, which resulted in tragedy. If his team fell apart, everyone would be lost. Because of this, Shackleton kept a constant vigil, looking for signs of eroding morale. His brilliance as a leader eventually contributed to all 27 of his men making it home in one piece.

While your team may not be involved in a life-or-death struggle, the principles of morale are just as valid. Work teams can be amazing environments for cooperation and group cohesion, or dysfunctional collections of individuals who would be better off working apart. The reason so much emphasis has been placed on the importance of teams stems back to our very origins as a species.

One of our primary psychological needs is to build emotional bonds with others. In fact, it's not just a psychological need, but a biological need as well. Our brain chemistry is wired for connection. Apparently, the lesson is that we need each other. Since the dawn of humanity, the lone wolves among us have continually been weeded out by natural selection, unless of course, they are not really alone. From our earliest days we have understood that there is safety in numbers, and our fear of being alone is universal. Because of this, each of us finds security and a host of other good things within a group. Connection with others also helps us find meaning and purpose. Apart from time with family and friends, we spend most of our lives at work. It is here where we need to find meaningful connection. Groups unleash powerful social forces that influence our behavior. Great managers understand this and give careful thought to protecting and building their team.

My next-door neighbor recently resigned from her job. She simply couldn't stand it anymore. It wasn't the job that she hated; it was the team she had to work with. When she submitted her resignation, the CEO of this small company was shocked. When he asked her why she was leaving, she informed him of certain people on the team whom she could no longer tolerate. He was oblivious to the problem. Although he was aware of undesirable behavior demonstrated by one of the staff members, he had minimized the impact on everyone else's morale. In doing so, he had lost a great employee while keeping the problematic individual around, effectively weakening his team.

A healthy team will provide an inspiring work environment, while a dysfunctional one will quickly erode morale and engagement. Being able to keep your pulse on the overall esprit de corps is a critical function of your role. But it is not only about keeping an eye on team morale; it is also about doing the little things consistently that will foster a functional and healthy team environment week in and week out. When your team is healthy and united, it provides a fertile environment for your employees. Healthy teams add to engagement and can increase motivation among individual members. Building a team takes focus and effort, and it often gets lost in the daily minutiae of work. The key is to make teams sticky. The stickier the team, the more effective it will be. There are certain principles that act like glue, pulling people together, while other principles act as solvents, eroding the very ties that bind. Sticky teams use lots of glue and keep the solvents far away.

TEAM GLUE

There are three major principles that hold a team together. They are purpose, trust, and ownership. A discussion of these principles follows.

Purpose

Any sticky team must center on something larger than itself. There must be a reason to exist. Teams that are merely individuals who happen to be organized together for reporting purposes are really not teams at all. They may be a group, but groups lack the motivational power that teams possess. If this describes your current environment (groups as opposed to teams), then understand that there will be limits to the kind of team you can build. There are still merits to giving some attention to team building from a relational and workplace enrichment perspective, but beyond that, extra time spent on team building will have limited success.

Teams, like people, want to achieve something. When a team is working toward a target or goal, that target or goal provides a focal point for its efforts. It is easier to lay aside egos and personalities when there is a larger goal toward which everyone is striving. Csíkszentmihályi's work on flow has some bearing here. Teams, like individual people, need a clear expectation or goal, a challenge that requires team members to work together. And they need consistent feedback to help them monitor their progress. What is your team trying to accomplish right now? Do team members have a common goal they are working toward? If so, do they know what it is? Do they know exactly where they are? The answers to these questions provide the glue that sticks people together. When it comes to building a team, think about soccer—not golf—where everyone's efforts contribute to a shared goal. Whenever you can create an environment of shared success, it helps people find purpose and feel relied upon by others. This social connection ignites a desire to contribute while not letting others down. Contribution scratches our itch for significance and is rooted in our need for connection and the safety that groups have always brought us as a species. Part of your job as a manager is to continually remind your team of its purpose and goals. By regularly keeping the goal in front of team members, you help the edges of your team stay glued together.

Trust

Your job as a manager is not to make everyone like each other. Teams that have a natural chemistry and seem to "click" do have an advantage. But, more than friendship, teams need to swim in an ocean of trust and respect. Trust, as we learned earlier, is the currency in which you as a leader must deal. The same goes for the team. In order to work together, walls must be broken down. When people trust one another, they will bring more of themselves to the team, be more committed to its success, and will be eager to support individual members. In a trusting environment people feel safe, and when they do, they will share more ideas, speak up when they disagree, and address concerns without fear of people taking it personally.

What kills a team is the fear of judgment, which springs from a lack of respect. This lack of respect will manifest itself in behaviors such as gossip—the meeting after the meeting—belittling of others' opinions, secret eye rolling, and a lack of truth telling. If any one these behaviors currently exists on your team, you probably have trust and respect issues. Once, during an expedition, I wandered off from base camp in order to spend a little time by myself. I made the mistake of not telling anyone where I was going. As I returned, the rest of the team was already in the cook tent, chowing down on dinner. John, our lead guide, saw me coming and caught up with me before I got to the tent. He gave me a short lecture on leaving base camp without telling anyone and then told me I had demonstrated a lack of respect for the cook and the other climbers. While I was a bit surprised initially by what he had said, I realized that he was right. It was disrespectful, even though it wasn't intentional. When I got to the tent I apologized to the cook and the rest of the team who just laughed and said it was no big deal. But John was right. By pointing out that I need to respect the team, he was making sure that disrespect did not get a foothold in our camp.

Another sign that trust may be low on your team is an absence of conflict. I'm not talking about relational or personality conflicts, but conflicts over process. When people feel that they can have respectful disagreements over process, it is healthy and conducive to innovation and creativity. A team full of quiet compliers will have mediocre performance at best. When team members trust each other, they are able to have lively discussions and actively disagree with one another. When individuals feel that they can share their opinions, thoughts, and concerns without the fear of isolation, teams become sticky. Creating an environment like this has more to do with you, the leader, than anyone else. Do your team members engage in lively discussions? Do team members feel that they can speak up and respectfully share their thoughts, ideas, and opinions? If not, you may want to investigate why and work on building more trust and respect.

Ownership Through Clarity and Accountability
A third principle of effective teams is ownership. When members of a team fail to step up and take responsibility for their part, it destroys morale. "All for one and one for all" is apparently a good motto for teams. Sometimes employees fail to take ownership because of a lack of clarity and/or accountability regarding their role. Team members must know exactly what is expected of them. It also helps when they can see how their performance affects everyone else. When roles and assignments are clear, then it is easy to hold everyone accountable. Accountability is an important tool in pulling teams together and in inspiring performance. When individual members are held to their commitments, it sends the message that everyone must pull his or her own weight. This further promotes a sense of equality, inspiring people to engage more freely.

SOLVENTS THAT THREATEN YOUR TEAM
While purpose, trust, and ownership all act to stick people together, each of these can quickly be undone by any number of solvents. The problem with solvents is they can dissolve the bonds formed by glue in half the time it took to build them. While much of team building focuses on adding more glue to the structure, a manager must pay even more attention to the solvents that erode the bonds of teamwork.

Ernest Shackleton realized that protecting a team's morale needs to be a top priority. As the crew of the *Endurance* learned, the biggest danger to the team was not the frigid temperatures or shifting ice floes, but rather, certain types of behaviors that could adversely affect morale. As a manager, people expect you to deal with these, and, if you fail to do so, you will likely lose some of the trust team members have placed in you as a leader. Even worse, some of your best people may resign—as my next-door neighbor did—to search for a happier, more functional team to join.

Problem Behaviors

The following types of people are better viewed as "behaviors." Behavior can be shaped, molded, and changed, and it is always good to view problem staff members in this way. They are not so much problem people as they are employees who demonstrate problem behavior. If any of these behaviors are present among the members of your staff, they will need your immediate attention.

The Slacker Nobody wants to be taken advantage of. We are very sensitive to situations that seem unfair. In fact, many employees have expressed that they want a "boss who is fair." We expect there to be fairness in the workplace, and while we may not know how much each of our coworkers makes, we have a general idea of how hard some of them work. When a team member is known to be a slacker and gets away with it, it severely undermines the motivation of everyone else. This is amplified when people fail to see any attempt by management to do anything about it. Employees can begin to question why the slacker is being paid the same as they are for half the amount of effort. While the employee cannot control how much the slacker is being paid, they can control how hard they, personally, want to work. In such a situation, even the best-hearted employees are tempted to say to themselves, "Why should I work twice as hard for the same amount of money? That's not fair." Under such situations, employees are tempted to lower their own level of engagement to eliminate the injustice. What inadvertently happens is that the standard of your team begins to drop to the level set by the slacker. On your team, a slacker will hurt motivation more than a hard worker will boost it. You must deal with the slacker.

The Skunk I grew up on a ranch, and I remember when a family of skunks decided to move in under our chicken coop. As skunks are known to kill chickens, this is not a good situation, so we went about getting rid of our new smelly friends. Skunks are amazing creatures, but as you know, they pack a potent defense mechanism—their spray. From time to time, one of our dogs would get sprayed by a skunk, and the scent would linger around the ranch for days. It was awful. You soon learn to keep your distance from skunks because you're afraid of them "going off."

Skunks in the workplace are no different. They are those difficult coworkers around whom you must walk on eggshells because you don't want to set them off. They constantly have their defenses up, and they are kings and queens of drama. In a way they resemble emotional terrorists, holding everyone hostage by their negative attitudes, defensiveness, and mood swings. Skunks are the people everyone knows to avoid, and they are probably the least-liked people on your team. A manager can't avoid or ignore a skunk any more than a farmer can. Failure to do so is unfair to the rest of your employees. Talk to the skunks about their ineffective behaviors and outline exactly what you want to change. Dealing with skunks is usually never a one-time occurrence. They need firm direction and accountability. Oh, and be prepared to be sprayed yourself.

The Whiner Nobody likes a complainer. Not even a complainer likes a complainer. Although studies have shown that pessimism can actually shorten your life, there is still no shortage of people who see the glass as half-empty. Having a complainer or pessimist on your team is like bringing a mourner to an Irish wake. My wife is Irish and, when her uncle died, her family gathered together for a good old-fashioned wake. It seems that even in death the Irish have found a way to party. The partying came to an end, however, when a well-wishing neighbor dropped by, sobbing and passing on condolences to the family.

"Thanks," they politely replied, but what they really meant was, "Thanks for ruining the party."

Whiners dampen the spirit and mood of a group. They kill fun and even destroy creativity. The problem with pessimism is that it has deep roots, and people who are pessimists usually do not change overnight. If you have pessimists or complainers on your team, forget about trying to change them. While they *can* learn to be more optimistic, leave that to them and their therapist. Your job is to minimize their destructive behavior. To do this, you have to identify the behaviors that elicit pessimism and give them some suggestions of alternate responses. Over time, you can at least minimize their negative effect on the rest of the team.

The Bully Bullies dominate the playground and make everyone else feel small. They like to be in control and get their own way. Bullies tend to believe that they are right all the time, and they force their opinions on others while trivializing everyone else's. A bully who is not dealt with will continue to squash your team spirit and rob you of great ideas and input. Often, bullies are not trying to be mean; they just haven't learned to tone down their personalities. If you have a bully on your team, be prepared to roll up your sleeves and tackle the problem behavior.

How to Address Problem Behavior

As a manager, one of your roles is to protect the team from any of the above behaviors. Any of them can pose a serious risk to the morale of your team and, because you are the leader, your direct reports expect you to deal with them. Whenever faced with a slacker, a skunk, a whiner, or a bully, remember this simple procedure for dealing with them:

1. *Behavior, behavior, behavior.* Always start by outlining the behavior they are exhibiting that needs to change. By focusing on the behavior itself, you avoid judgmental statements that will only escalate emotions and make matters worse. For example, let's say one of

your staff members is a slacker. We'll call him Joey. Joey is always abusing his breaks, coming in late, and taking a longer lunch than anyone else. Joey's laziness is affecting team morale. While it might feel good to say to Joey, "You're lazy," it is not going to help you in the long run. By staying away from judgmental statements such as this, you are able to focus on the behavior in question, which is that Joey abuses his lunch breaks and comes to work late.

2. *Consequence.* After you have identified the problem behavior, help the employee understand the consequences of his or her actions. In Joey's case there are many consequences to choose from. When Joey abuses his lunch break, his coworkers disrespect him, which means that it will be hard to promote him to higher levels of responsibility. Another possible consequence is that his example discourages other team members and lowers overall work ethic. Maybe Joey's lateness affects the productivity of the team, putting everyone else behind schedule. The point here is to link Joey's behavior to a real consequence within the work environment.

3. *Direction.* After you have identified their behavior and tied it to a consequence, tell them what you want them to do or what you want them to stop doing.

Giving corrective feedback does not need to take a long time and is better when it is done quickly and professionally. No one wants to be lectured for 20 minutes on anything. Most problem behaviors will not change right away, but if you consistently address the behavioral issues—discouraging the inappropriate behaviors while encouraging the effective ones—you will either see the desired changes or the problem personality will eventually leave.

MORE GLUE

One of the intangible ways to increase trust and boost morale is to increase social cohesion among your team members. Social cohesion is the glue that bonds people relationally. There is merit in bringing people together and helping them connect on a friendship level. For members who are more socially gifted, connecting with one another is easy. For others, like the more task-focused personalities, relationships require a bit more work. This is where you as a leader come in. Serving as a catalyst, you can create environments where people can interact and learn more about each other. Making these connections increases the bonds of trust and feelings of goodwill among your staff members. To do this, you do not need a fancy and expensive team-building day. The best relational teams are built with small interactions week in and week out. It takes a bit of creativity and initiative on your part.

Paul's Army

Paul was a manager I coached who wanted to increase the team spirit among his employees. We brainstormed for a bit, and then Paul came up with a simple idea. He decided that for the next month, all 10 of his team members would meet in his office at 8:00 a.m. every Wednesday morning. From there, he would lead them outside and off to a different specialty coffee shop where they would spend the next 45 minutes discussing anything but work. The rules were simple: you had to be in his office by 8:00 a.m. or else you wouldn't know which coffee house the team had gone to. Paul would buy you whatever you wanted, and you could talk about anything but work. Paul's once-a-week coffee outing took on a name of its own as his employees named it "Paul's Army," because of his regimented 8:00 a.m. start time. If you showed up late, you missed out.

Paul's simple idea quickly became a hit, not only with his team but with other teams as well. Soon another manager was approached by his team members asking if they could do something similar, and then a third manager was asked by her team if they could do something together as well. A cynical boss might see this exercise as nothing more than employees trying to get out of work. For some this might be true, but the majority of your employees desire to be able to connect with others, especially those they work with. I had a chance to ask one of Paul's direct reports almost six months later about Paul's experiment. A big smile came across her face. "We had so much fun," she beamed. "We just laughed and laughed." It is hard to put a dollar amount on statements like that, and it is no wonder that Paul had a stellar retention rate among his employees. Of course, Paul didn't even need to leave the office. They could have done the same thing in someone's cubicle. The point is that people crave connection, and sometimes they just need a catalyst to get the ball rolling.

The Meteorologist and the Scrapbooker

Keeping an eye on team morale can be difficult for some managers. Not everyone is gifted with the ability to read the climate. One idea I often pass on to managers is to appoint someone on your team as your meteorologist. We are all familiar with meteorologists on the news. They are trained to read the climate and predict what's coming. Some people have this gift when it comes to relationships. They are able to read people well, and they seem to feel even the tiniest disruptions to workplace morale. Having someone on your team like this can be a huge asset. If you are so lucky, then you might want to ask that person to be your meteorologist; paying extra attention to team morale and informing you of anything you might be missing. Of course, I am not talking about appointing a spy or a snitch. Simply someone who feels he or she has the freedom to pull you aside and say, "I think the team is pretty discouraged about the recent layoffs over in the finance department."

One of my bosses early in my career taught me the power of building memories. Memories, at least good ones, are powerful things. They are snapshots from the past that evoke positive emotions and remind people of the bonds they share. Memories are important to teams. The problem with memories is that they mostly lie dormant until there is a catalyst to arouse them. Whether it is a coworker saying, "Remember the time we . . ." or a photograph of the team lunch six months ago that gets circulated, such triggers help bond teams and add to morale. Even bad times can form good memories if there's enough distance of time from the actual event. Think about the last time you went camping and the tent leaked. Such misery usually becomes something to laugh about later down the road.

To help tap into the power of the past, appoint someone on the team as the official scrapbooker. This person's task is simply to make sure that pictures are taken and good times are captured and then later circulated. In several not-for-profit organizations I led in the past, I would always have an end-of-year banquet to thank the staff and volunteers. We would usually finish the night with a slideshow made up of pictures and videos gathered throughout the year. We would set it to music and make sure that everyone made it onto the big screen. It was always a favorite part of the night, as people were treated to a collage of images invoking powerful memories of the past year. After it was over and the lights came on, there was usually no shortage of teary-eyed people. The memories of the year were there, but, lying dormant, they had little emotional impact. The slide show served as a trigger to unlock those good feelings and remind people of what a fantastic team we all belonged to.

PROTECTING NEW HIRES

Imagine being born a zebra. The African savanna makes the bad part of town look like Disneyland. The minute you enter the world, you are in danger. Lions, cheetahs, and hyenas lurk in the distance, scanning the herd for weak, sick, and young individuals. The first hours of a young zebra's life are critical. Their survival hinges on two very important things. The first is their ability to stand up on their own feet quickly. Lions have not yet heard of giving zebras a running start. The other essential is their ability to pick their mother out of a crowd. If you thought distinguishing between your neighbor's identical twins was tough, imagine picking your mother out of a lineup of 100 women, all of whom look the same at first glance. Knowing who your mother is on the African savanna is a survival issue because during your first days of life she is your lifeline and food source.

Fortunately for zebras, nature has provided them with a simple way around this problem. It's called imprinting. After a mother zebra gives birth to a foal, she will stand between it and the rest of the herd, preventing it from seeing anyone but her. During this time her foal imprints its mother's stripe pattern and smell so it will always be able to find her in a crowd. This imprinting is essential for the zebra's survival.

Just as a zebra herd has its strategies for protecting its young, so should organizations when it comes to their new hires. One study found that a whopping 25 percent of new hires will quit within the first year. In order to avoid the cost and consequences of new hire resignations, many organizations have designed on-boarding initiatives. Such on-boarding programs are necessary, and most HR departments have either rolled one out or are in the process of crafting one. These programs vary across organizations, and there is plenty of information out there to help you create one. The challenge with some on-boarding processes is that they are too academic and task-oriented. Although well-meaning, these types of programs (usually contained in a large binder) merely teach employees about their benefit packages and whom to talk to if they need assistance in a certain area. What such programs lack is the power to stick people to the herd. While getting a tour of the facilities and a welcome lunch with the CEO is helpful, it doesn't necessarily bond the new hire emotionally. When new hires bond emotionally with your workplace, it creates a powerful connection that will increase their sense of ownership and belonging. This connection is forged by helping new hires create four distinctive bonds:

1. *Bond with you.* The number-one reason why people leave their jobs is unhappiness with management. As we learned earlier, you as

a manager carry incredible influence in the lives of your direct reports. While your longtime employees enjoy a relationship with you that has been built over time, new hires are starting from scratch. Your connection with them requires some consistent effort. This is why it's important to free up space in your schedule whenever you hire someone new. By carving out regular time for new employees, they get to know who you are, learn what you expect, and have an opportunity to see that you care (see Chapter 5). Your relationship with them will do more to determine their satisfaction and happiness at work than any other single thing. Making time available in your schedule, especially early on, will help build trust between you and your new hire.

2. *Bond with the team.* While most teams take new hires out for a group lunch during the first week, little is done beyond that to pull them in to the group. It's not that people are unfriendly; they're just busy. Great relationships at work contribute to an employee's happiness and engagement. But not everybody is a natural when it comes to making new friends. In order to assist your new hires, a little bit of behind-the-scenes effort can work miracles. Each week try to pair up your new hire with one of your other employees. This can be as simple as getting the new hire to job shadow someone or by calling up Joe and asking him if he'll take the new employee for a lunch or coffee this week. Joe will probably be glad to help out but may not have initiated this without your prompting. By creating interactions between your team and the new hire, you help them forge emotional bonds that otherwise may have taken much longer to build.

3. *Bond with their role.* It is important that you help your new hires see the link between their performance and its effect on the company. The quicker and more clearly you can help create this line of sight, the more bonded to their role they become. If new hires' roles affect anyone else in the company, be sure they get a chance

to meet them face to face. For example, when your new hire, Bill, meets Diane and learns that his performance makes her job easier or more frustrating, it helps him create an emotional link to his performance. Or when Bill sees that his work has an impact on the entire team, the customer, or the organization as a whole, it helps him take more ownership of his work. When employees feel that they are being counted on, it helps them connect on a more emotional level with their role.

4. *Bond with the organization.* Bonding new hires to an organization is powerful but often overlooked. The quicker that new hires develop a sense of pride in their company, the better chances you have of keeping them. To do this, you have to help your new hires see that your company has a soul. When people see that it's not only about the money, they pay even more attention. While every organization has a balance sheet, sticky companies have much more to be proud of than simply profits.

Giving Back

Many organizations do a great job of giving back to their communities and involving themselves in worthy causes. This needs to be highlighted early and often. If there is any way to get your new hires personally involved in some of your company's charitable work, it will increase the pride they feel about your company.

Corporate Stories and Highlights

Awards and special kinds of recognition that your company has received are also nice to show off but a story is better than a trophy. Stories about your organization's history bring it to life, especially when they communicate your values and culture. If you get a job at Carmichael Lynch, an ad agency in Minneapolis, you will undoubtedly get a chance to see the Mitsubishi conference room. There you will find a crumpled-up heap of metal underneath a piece of glass which acts as a coffee table. The story behind the table is this. Apparently, Carmichael Lynch pitched Mitsubishi and was rejected, so the team members had a Mitsubishi car crushed while they all went out to watch. Now it is their coffee table. The story instantly paints a picture of an edgy, fun culture and inspires most people to say, "Wow, that's cool!" Find your cool stories and pass them on to your new hires. It brings your organization to life.

Social Highlights

Most workplaces have their own traditions and special events. Having a photo album on hand to show some of these is a great idea. This is especially powerful if you tie it into the team lunch. The laughter brought about by shared memories will definitely leave an impression on your new employee.

It's a Family Affair

One of the best ways to protect a new hire is to get the entire team involved. Before your new hire starts, have a planning session with your team, brainstorming different ways you can all get involved in the onboarding process. You can turn this into a bit of a team-building event itself. Invoke some team pride and identity by proclaiming that no other team in the company will do as good a job as your team in welcoming a new employee. This stake in the ground will inspire both pride and ownership in the team members.

The key to bonding your new hires is, once again, awareness. New hires go through a gamut of emotions and challenges during their first few weeks on the job. The more you can do to help them bond emotionally to their workplace, the greater the chances are that they will stick around.

SUMMARY

A team is an important part of most workplaces, and as a leader you must always keep one finger on the pulse of group morale. Building a team does not have to involve massive interruptions to everyone's schedule or expensive off-site team-building activities. The best teams are built day by day, meeting by meeting, and memory by memory. By rallying around a common purpose, fostering trust and respect, and promoting ownership through clarity and accountability, your team can protect itself from the destructive problem behaviors that potentially destroy the effectiveness of a group. In your nine-minute planning time take a moment to consider what you can do this week to add more stickiness to your team.

MINUTE SEVEN SUMMARY

Key Lessons

- Teams are founded on:
  1. Purpose
  2. Trust
  3. Ownership
- Protecting your team from problem behaviors is paramount.
- Use social bonding to increase team stickiness.
- Protect your new hires by bonding them emotionally to:
  1. You
  2. Your team
  3. Your organization
  4. Their role

Key Question

- What can I do to make my team stickier this week?

Key Action Step

- Go to www.nineminutesonmonday.com and download the "sticky team" inventory.

• MINUTE 7 •

What can I do to make my team
stickier this week?

Laughter in the Funeral Home
The Need to Play

I never did a day's work in my life. It was all fun.

—Thomas Edison

The funeral home was quiet when I walked in. Come to think of it, funeral homes are always quiet. I was there to meet a man named Michael Pierson, the director of Pierson Funeral Homes. I had one burning question on my mind that I wanted an answer to. Do the people who work in funeral homes have any fun?

Few jobs would seem more serious than working in a funeral home. Helping people say good-bye to loved ones by providing them with a dignified and respectful service is one of the most important jobs on the planet. But if you are like me, it doesn't look like a fun place to work. In fact, from the outside it would seem like a downright depressing place to spend 40 hours a week. After all, you are constantly dealing with grieving families, incredibly serious situations, and dead bodies. So do funeral home employees actually have any fun? This mystery led me to interview a funeral home director for a segment I was doing about fun in the workplace.

When I asked about the importance of having fun at work, Michael Pierson assured me, "It's critical." He went on to tell me, "Not losing sight of the seriousness of what we do, we *have* to have fun."

Michael spoke to me about the necessary role that fun plays in helping employees get through the day, while they are working as quickly and efficiently as they can. He went on to say that having a bit of fun actually helps employees do a better job serving their clients. Fun in such an environment acts almost like an antidote, counteracting the stress and emotional load placed on each staff member. So if funeral home workers are allowed to have a little fun at work, how about the rest of us?

FUN AND PRODUCTIVITY

One of the biggest knocks against fun at work is that it seems to be the polar opposite of productivity. Probably most of us can look back on jobs we had in high school where we may have goofed off. When I worked at the golf course as a teenager with six of my buddies, racing golf carts was not part of the job description, but we found a way to make it happen. Although it was a lot of fun, we didn't get much work done. Fun, like anything, can be abused but, believe it or not, a dose of fun actually increases productivity. The reasons for this are many, the least of which is humor's powerful effect on stress.

According to the American Institute of Stress, job stress is far and away the biggest source of anxiety for American adults, and it has gotten worse over the last few decades. Work-related stress has been linked to increased rates of heart attack, hypertension, and other disorders. In fact, in major cities such as New York, the relationship between job stress and heart attacks is so well documented that any police officer who suffers a heart attack on or *off* the job is assumed to have a work-related injury and is compensated accordingly.

Many companies today make workplace safety a top priority, spending millions of dollars training and educating their workers. Injuries on a work site can have a devastating effect on a person's life, and they also disrupt productivity. But the damage caused by stress, both in employees' lives and productivity loss to the organization, easily matches, if not exceeds, the toll from physical injuries. One study found that nearly eight out of ten workplace injuries were stress related. Stress not only causes physical injuries such as heart attacks, it also has a rippling emotional effect. Stressed-out workers perform more poorly, have a greater propensity to take their frustration out on a fellow employee, and are more likely to quit. Yet stress reduction is not given a fraction of the attention that is directed to the more obvious safety concerns that exist in a workplace. When is the last time you saw a poster at work counting how many stress-free injury days there were in your workplace? One of the problems is that we've begun to accept a certain number of stress-related injuries as the norm. It may be true that Jack chewed out Andy a little too harshly, but give him a break; he's under a lot of stress.

The good news about the poison created by stress is that there are a couple of antivenoms to counteract its toxicity, one of which is fun. If you want to keep a lid on stress at work, make sure you inject a little fun once in a while. Like an IV drip, even the smallest doses of fun can take the edge off the harmful effects of stress. Laughter, it turns out, releases pleasurable endorphins, lowers our blood pressure, and helps us tolerate more pain. The manager who thinks that fun at work decreases productivity has failed to look at the evidence. It seems that the funeral home director was right when he told me that having fun at work is critical.

Another way that fun will boost your productivity is that it actually increases the number of days your employees will spend at work. Fun and laughter at work have been linked to less absenteeism and fewer sick days. While stress has a dampening effect on our immune system, fun and laughter actually give it a boost, protecting us from illness. And if you still need more convincing, laughter actually increases our tolerance for pain. In the presence of painful stimuli, fun helps us endure.

FUN ADDS TO CREATIVITY

Michael Kerr is a good friend of mine and happens to be one of the world's leading experts on humor in the workplace. He is also a highly-sought-after speaker on the subject. According to Michael, humor at work is serious business. Without it, your staff will not be as creative, or as motivated as they are with it. Creativity is necessary for any organization to continue to evolve. More than ever, companies depend on innovation to help them stay ahead of the competition. There's a reason why children have so many ideas. They spend most of their day playing. Having fun puts us into a different brain space from, say, crunching numbers for the monthly report. When your people are having fun, they are more likely to come up with great ideas that are going to help improve effectiveness. Fun can also break up the monotony of routine tasks. Most people have certain aspects of their job that are monotonous and/or mindless. Humor has a way of giving the mind a break, as if sending it to the spa. Having a little fun can refresh your wiring, enabling you to jump back into the task with renewed energy.

FUN PROTECTS YOUR TEAM

In the last chapter we talk about the importance of creating sticky teams. One of the strongest glues that bring people together is laughter. "Humor in the workplace," says Kerr, "keeps the mood light and maintains a climate of positive energy, which helps keep morale high." When morale is strong, teams function better because coworkers get along. Fun and laughter have a way of diffusing tense times around the office, and a good laugh can help everyone gain some much needed perspective. It's hard to have conflict with those you regularly laugh with. When coworkers like each other, they are more likely to expend extra effort to help the team. Remember Paul's army from Chapter 11? When I asked one of his direct reports about it, she smiled and, with glowing eyes, told me how much fun it was. The team that plays together stays together.

FUN IMPROVES COMMUNICATION

Communication in the workplace is key. The fewer the barriers, the more easily information flows. We have already talked at length about how trust is imperative to great communication. But humor also plays a huge role. Michael Kerr emphasizes that humor and fun in the workplace open the lines of communication. Humor breaks down barriers and puts people at ease. TV sitcoms that are taped before a live studio audience usually open up with a comedian who spends a few minutes warming up the audience. Sitting among a group of strangers has an inhibiting effect on people. It makes them more reserved, cautious, and less engaging with each other. After the comedian is through, the collective mood has changed. Laughing with a bunch of strangers has a powerful effect on a person's perception of the group. Laughter forms tiny bonds that increase one's comfort level and opens up channels of communication. When people feel comfortable with each other, communication has fewer barriers.

FUN AS A STRATEGIC TOOL

Earlier in this book we talked about the importance of maintaining awareness as a leader. It's important to keep an eye on your group's pace of travel. By pace of travel, I mean the overall level of activity and stress at any given time. Most workplaces go through cycles of intensely busy times followed by short lulls where everyone tries to catch his breath. As a leader you want to be in tune with this. When the team has been pushing hard for an extended period of time, people get tired, nerves get frayed, and stress levels rise. It is during times like these where fun can have a profound impact.

Whenever your team has been working extra hard, making time for play is critical, even if it is only in small doses. It could be a team lunch where no one is allowed to talk about work, or as simple as a knock-knock joke-telling contest at a team meeting. The point is that as a manager you want to keep your pulse on the pace of travel of your group. When things have been crazy busy for a while, it is definitely time for some fun. In this way, fun becomes a strategic component to help protect the team and motivate the troops.

FUN AS A VITAL SIGN

One of the most striking things Michael Kerr said to me when we spoke is that he sees humor as an indicator of the health of a workplace. Humor, he says, is not so much something you add to a workplace as it is a sign of the many things already going well. Humor, fun, and laughter, then, act as a sort of gauge of workplace health. A lack of fun and humor at work are signs that something is amiss. As a manager, you will benefit by lightening up and adding more fun at work on a regular basis. There is definitely a time and place where adding fun into the work environment is the strategic thing to do.

Some work environments are more difficult than others from a motivational standpoint. Some jobs don't provide a connection to purpose; others fail to meet one's need for achievement. In environments such as these, fun can be injected to increase the enjoyment of work. When some of the deeper needs discussed in this book are not being met, fun can act as a sort of salve. Sitting in a parking lot pay station for 40 hours a week becomes a lot more bearable when your manager tries to add a little fun to the job.

FLYING FISH

When I was a teenager, my parents took me on a trip to Seattle, Washington. I have only a few memories of the vacation. I remember riding in a limousine for the first time, watching a Mariners game in the old King Dome, and visiting a crowded market where men were throwing fish through the air while onlookers stopped to watch the show. Mackerel were being heaved over the heads of customers; salmon were used like puppets, welcoming you to Seattle, while employees laughed, joked, and entertained the crowd. Years later this same fish market would become world famous and spawned an entire workplace philosophy, teaching organizations about the importance of having fun at work.

A couple of years ago I revisited the famous fish market, but this time not as a tourist. I wanted to interview one of the employees and see if the workers were still having fun. It was there that I met Sam, one of the frontline workers scheduled to work that day. I asked him about the importance of having fun at work, and he responded by telling me that, "Having fun makes the job easier." When I asked him if he had any advice for managers who might think that fun is not something that belongs in the workplace, he said, "Tell them to relax. It's your workers. You have to treat them well because if you don't treat them right, they're not going to be as productive and they won't want to come to work." Sam capped off our interview by telling me, "It starts with the boss. If the boss has fun, everyone has fun."

Even though my interview with Sam lasted all of one minute, he summarized the importance of fun at work quite well: Fun makes the job easier. If you treat your employees right, they will be more productive. Bosses should relax a bit. And if *you*, the boss, have some fun, your employees will have fun too.

IT STARTS WITH THE BOSS

With all of this evidence that having fun at work is a good thing, why are there still so many workplaces not having it? Sam, the fishmonger from Seattle, provided a big part of the answer when he said, "It starts with the boss." As a leader, you become the ceiling in a variety of areas, and fun at work is one of them. A boss who allows herself to loosen up and have a little fun is giving the rest of her employees permission to do the same. Have you ever worked for a boss who was serious all the time? Was it much fun? Probably not. Many of your employees will take their cues from you as to what is appropriate and what's not. If you like to laugh, it allows them the freedom to laugh as well.

However, loosening up is hard for some managers. Part of this is the result of the extra responsibility placed on them. Managers are held accountable for the work that gets accomplished by their teams. This extra responsibility carries with it the potential for higher levels of stress. Our natural response as managers when we are stressed is to constrict and work harder. While we work to make progress, we forget to lighten up and have fun along the way. It's not easy to be a catalyst for fun when things are hectic, but doing so actually helps our staff members do their jobs more effectively. Another reason why managers find it hard to lighten up is the false perception regarding their role. They feel that people will not respect them or take them seriously if they are not serious. Humor at work is not an all-or-nothing thing. While it is possible to lose respect by coming across as goofy, no one is asking you to do that. The key is to be able to lighten up enough to allow others the freedom to have a little fun.

An added benefit of humor in the workplace is that it helps build trust and rapport between you and your direct reports. It does this by lessening the distance between you and your employees that is created by the authority of your position. Humor will make you seem more relatable to your direct reports. In this way it helps you increase the bonds of trust.

I'm Just Not That Funny

The good news is that you do not have to become a comedian to add a little fun to your workplace. Comedy and jokes are not the sole definition of fun. Remember, the ability to have fun at work starts with an attitude to lighten up and stop taking everything so seriously. One of the most powerful things you can do is to laugh at yourself. The ability to laugh at oneself is an admirable trait. It signifies humility, which draws people to you. Instead of covering up mistakes or challenges, find the lighter side of these moments. Your staff will love you for it.

Safe Humor

One of the concepts that Michael Kerr stresses during his humor at work presentations is the need for safe humor. He advises managers to avoid telling jokes, especially dirty ones, and instead focus on telling funny stories. Another tip is to stay away from any humor that pokes fun at race, religion, gender, or disability. While this may seem obvious, there are countless incidents of managers who offend their staff with inappropriate jokes. This can be especially true in a male-dominated work environment. Humor at work must be respectful and free of sexual innuendos. Such jokes make many women feel uncomfortable and should be avoided at all costs. One joke in poor taste can damage the trust you have worked so hard to build. Kerr says to practice the first rule of safe humor, which is to laugh at yourself.

Meetings

One of the easiest places to add fun at work is during your meetings. Most of the workforce seems to loathe meetings and for good reason. When meetings have no agenda, go on too long, involve too many people, and result in no decisions being made, it's easy to see why so many view them as a waste of time. But meetings, done correctly, can be a great place to build team, to teach and train, and most importantly to this chapter, have fun. Your options for how to add fun to your meetings are limited only by your creativity. Humor and fun are powerful in small doses. Even by taking a minute or two during each meeting to laugh and blow off some steam will have positive results. Your staff members do not need to be falling over themselves laughing to benefit. Next time you have a meeting with your staff, think of a simple way you can laugh a little.

Humor to Soothe Pain

It has already been noted that laughter can actually increase your tolerance for pain. One organization I heard about used humor to help its staff deal with particularly unpleasant work situations such as handling nasty customers. I remember hearing of a bank that held a weekly contest among its bank tellers for "worst customer of the week." At the end of each week tellers would share their experience in dealing with a particularly difficult customer. Then one was chosen as the worst customer, and a prize was given to the employee. Of course the actual customers were never informed (although maybe they should have been), but this is a great example of how humor can be used in the workplace. Dealing with a nasty customer is no fun. But imagine how your perception changes when your nasty customer just may get you a prize based on how well you handle the situation. The whole exercise gave the staff something to laugh about and turned potentially stressful situations into opportunities to shine and have fun.

Find Your Court Jester

In every team there is always somebody who seems funnier than the rest. Whether it's her outlook on life, her style of humor, or her flair for either the dramatic or the unexpected, she has a knack for creating contagious fun. If you have someone on your team who fits this description, then by all means make sure you let her use her gift. Giving the court jester the room to have a little fun takes enormous pressure off you and provides a constant source of smiles and laughs among the rest of the group. Such people are huge morale boosters. Be sure to use the recognition codes from Chapter 7 to help the jesters see how valuable a role they play in the team. Chances are, no one has ever before helped them see the link between their humor and how much it adds to the team.

Appoint a Director of Fun

Another idea is to find someone on your team who exudes fun and appoint this person as your director of fun (DOF). Let the employee know that one of her new responsibilities is to help the team have more fun. Be sure to provide the limits and then let her go. Fun people will love this role and be a great asset to your team. This will also take some of the load off you, leaving you time to focus on other things. Just remember that appointing a director of fun doesn't get you off the hook for cracking a few smiles yourself. You need them as much, if not more, than your direct reports.

Having fun at work will help your team get more done, have better relationships, find more creative ideas, and increase the relational bonds of your team. By leading the way in this area, you give your staff the permission to lighten up and have a little fun themselves. During your leadership planning time, take a minute to become aware of the current pace of travel and stress levels among the group. If things have been tense lately, you want to consider how you might inject some humor into the schedule during the week. Even if things are moving along at a manageable pace, think of one thing you can do this week to add a little fun to your workplace.

MINUTE EIGHT SUMMARY

Key Lessons

- Fun at work is serious business.
- Fun:
  - Increases productivity
  - Inspires creativity
  - Improves communication
  - Builds trust
  - Protects the team
- It starts with the boss.

Key Question

- Where can I inject some fun this week?

Key Action Step

- Visit www.mikekerr.com and sign up for Michael's weekly newsletter to get fresh ideas on adding fun to your workplace.

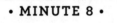

• MINUTE 8 •

*Where can I inject some fun
this week?*

Avatar
The Need for a Model

Follow me.

—Jesus

On April 18, 2010, a man named Hugo Alfredo Tale-Yax collapsed and lay dying on a sidewalk in Queens, New York. Over the next hour and twenty minutes, more than 25 people walked past and did nothing.

Mr. Tale-Yax was actually a Good Samaritan who ran to the aid of a woman being threatened by a knife-yielding man. Surveillance video from a nearby building captured Tale-Yax pursuing the assailant before collapsing on the sidewalk. The video clearly shows people walking by, some pausing to glance, and one man even stopping to take a picture with his cell phone. In tragic irony, Mr. Tale-Yax died because he saved a woman's life, while nobody stopped to help save his.

Even in New York, a city accustomed to street violence, the story outraged the citizens. The incident also brought back memories of the infamous murder of Kitty Genovese in Kew Gardens, also in Queens. In 1964 Catherine Genovese was attacked and killed outside her apartment. The struggle endured for more than 30 minutes, and her screams for help were heard by at least a dozen people, yet no one contacted the police. Most assumed someone else had already done so. This phenomenon led psychologists to open up a new field of study on what would later be called the Genovese syndrome, better known as the bystander effect.

There has been much debate about why people fail to help others in such situations but, through continued research, some interesting patterns have begun to emerge. It turns out that many of these situations are not as much issues of individual callousness as they are examples of the powers of social influence.

Two psychologists, Bibb Latané and John Darley, set out to explore the power of social influence and its effects on people. They designed a series of experiments where volunteers were exposed to situations in which someone suddenly needed help. In one study, while subjects completed written surveys, the room where they sat gradually began to fill up with smoke. In another, subjects heard a loud crash from the next room. This was immediately followed by a woman screaming, "Oh my God, my foot...I...I...can't move it! Oh my ankle. I can't get this thing off me!"

A third study had subjects participate in a group discussion over the intercom when one of the participants suddenly began to choke, gasp, and then call for help. All these studies demonstrated consistent findings. As the numbers of participants or "bystanders" increased, the likelihood that one of them would take action decreased. While the bystander effect is complex and multidimensional, there appears to be two main reasons why people in groups are slow, or even fail, to act.

The first one is the result of a diffusion of responsibility. The more people present, the less responsible one feels in any given situation. When a person witnesses someone in trouble and the witness is alone, there is a greater responsibility to act, whereas if ten individuals all see the same person who needs help, they are tempted to only feel one-tenth the responsibility. This diffusion of responsibility releases us from the compulsion to take action.

The second reason why people are slow to act is related to a concept called social proof. When faced with an ambiguous situation, people tend to scan the environment for feedback to gain clues as to how they should act. In the experiment where a loud crash came from an adjacent room, subjects would calmly glance at others' reactions to gauge whether or not they should be alarmed. Because everyone else in the room was doing the same thing, a strong social proof is established that there is nothing to worry about here. Because no one else seems concerned, to act would surely expose one person to a greater risk of social rejection, and because of our inherent need to connect with others, human beings generally avoid such risks.

You might be wondering what any of this has to do with leadership. People are heavily influenced by social forces. To help navigate this landscape, strong models are needed. In any of the above scenarios, if someone had leapt into action, many more would surely have followed. In a recent worldwide survey it was found that people are looking for inspirational and competent leaders. It seems that in an ever-changing world with a rather unstable economy, people want leaders who will make them feel secure and inspired. The same survey, however, also showed that confidence in today's leaders and managers is at an all-time low.

During times in which employee confidence has been shaken, a leader's example is paramount. Like returning to the gold standard during a recession, people look to models to follow when times are difficult. And right now employees want you to be inspirational. But when you ask an employee what an inspirational leader looks like, you are bound to get a variety of different answers. Before we resign inspiration to a hard-to-measure abstract concept, it is worth noting that there are a few common traits that seem to be present among those leaders we see as inspiring.

LEADERS WHO MODEL COURAGE

Imagine that you have signed up to participate in a psychology experiment. You are seated at a long table with a group of other volunteers who have been asked to examine cards like the one in Figure 4. The researcher then asks each one of you to pick which line on the right (A, B, or C) matches the line on the left. The researcher continues to cycle through different cards as the members of the group give their answers. Unbeknownst to you, the other volunteers are actually part of the experiment. The only real subject in this study is you. Things progress nicely until suddenly, on the next question—the one you see in the diagram—the other volunteers all choose C as their answer. This confuses you because it should be obvious to everyone that the correct answer is A. After everyone else has picked C, the researcher now looks at you. What answer do you give?

If you are like 75 percent of the actual people in this experiment, you defy your own eyes at least once and conform to the group by giving the incorrect answer. While this experiment demonstrates the incredible power of social conformity, a slight modification illustrates another powerful social principle.

In a variation of the experiment, a member of the study was planted in the middle of the group. This person would go against the rest by giving the correct response. When the real subject was asked to give his answer, he was no longer alone. With the presence of this nonconformist, the real subject conformed only one-fourth as often.

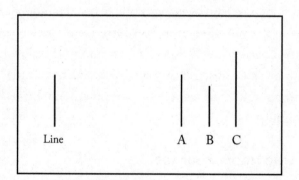

Figure 4

When someone else had the courage to be right, it actually strengthened the conviction of the real subject. People do not always carry the emotional strengths to be true to themselves. Leaders who are courageous enough to take a stand for what is right inspire others to take a stand as well. Leaders who are courageous inspire us because we are able to borrow some of their conviction in order to give legs to our own.

There are hundreds of stories throughout history of men and women who, because of their courage to stand up for something, helped others stay true to themselves. When Rosa Parks refused to give up her seat to a white person on a city bus in Montgomery, Alabama, in 1955, she had little idea it would spark the Montgomery bus boycott. Parks's courage became an important symbol in the civil rights movement. During that time there were undoubtedly many others who wanted to do what Rosa Parks did (and indeed some did), but it was the courage of one that inspired others to find their voice. Inspiring leaders help us find the strength to act (like running into the next room to see if the person the file cabinet fell on is okay).

LEADERS ELEVATE PERFORMANCE

Chef Gordon Ramsey might be best known for his TV show *Kitchen Nightmares*, where he spends a week inside a troubled restaurant attempting to turn it around. The scenario for each episode of *Kitchen Nightmares* follows a predictable pattern. Chef Ramsey visits the troubled eatery, tries the food, and then after spitting it out, proceeds to the kitchen to give the owners some honest feedback on what he really thinks. Ramsay inspects the kitchen and refrigerators for cleanliness and hygiene, looking for anything that would be considered substandard. By the end of the explosive hour, Chef Ramsey has used his experience and high standards to transform not only the restaurant but, more importantly, the owners themselves. The show usually ends with the owners' passion restored and running the restaurant with renewed energy and confidence. There is usually a moment at the end of every show when the transformed owners, while speaking to the camera, will say something like, "I just want to thank Chef Ramsey for getting me passionate again about food."

Although I would not recommend that you speak to your employees the way Gordon Ramsey addresses these restaurateurs on the show, there is an important leadership lesson to be learned here. Gordon Ramsey inspires people to elevate their game, and he does it by holding them to a consistently high standard.

When I ask participants in my leadership seminars to tell me about people in their past who have helped inspire them to do their best, I usually hear the same things over and over. One of the most common things shared is that those people who helped them had challenged them. We discussed earlier that a leader's ability to hold direct reports to a high standard is crucial. By setting a standard that is high, but not unrealistic, people are forced to find ways to outperform themselves. The challenge of holding your employees to a high standard is that it sometimes causes friction initially. This is long forgotten, though, once people achieve something extraordinary. It is usually at this point that they look back at you with a sense of gratitude and credit you with inspiring them to be their best. Of course, if you are going to hold your people to a standard of excellence, you first want to hold to it yourself. Ramsey has tasted success partly because of his high standards, and people know this. He has modeled excellence in the food industry, whether it be his cuisine or the cleanliness of his kitchen.

Holding staff members to a high standard can be difficult for some people. If you hate conflict and want your staff to merely like you, then you will probably have a fun but ineffective place to work. While caring for your people is essential, it should not come at the expense of standards. Leaders who are able to care while holding their staff to high standards make up that rare breed of managers whom others will deem inspirational.

LEADERS INSPIRE PASSION AND INCREASE ENERGY

When I was in my early twenties, a missionary from Malaysia came to visit the church I was attending. His purpose was clear. He wanted individuals who were born in Southeast Asia to consider moving back in order to help him with ongoing mission work. He was not a tall man, but what he lacked in height he made up for in passion and zeal. As I sat and listened to his presentation, I couldn't help but get excited. After 45 minutes, I wanted to move to Malaysia, not because there is anything in Kuala Lumpur that I wanted to see, but because I wanted to be in the presence of this guy. His passion and energy were captivating.

In England during the mid-1700s a preacher by the name of John Wesley helped spark a religious revival. When asked what brought the large crowds to hear him preach, he responded, "I am on fire with the Holy Spirit, and people come to watch me burn." Passion draws others to you.

People want to be a part of something that is worth getting excited about. If they don't see any passion in you, fat chance they are going to experience it themselves. Passion is contagious, and it increases energy in the workplace. When I speak of passion, I am not talking about becoming a missionary or a preacher, but rather I'm talking about becoming someone who is excited and committed to success. The simplest way to raise the energy level among your team members is to get truly excited about what you are doing. I remember coaching one manager who realized that he rarely brought much enthusiasm to the workplace. He simply decided to get more passionate about his work and excited about what his team was doing. By reconnecting with your own purpose and passion, you serve your team members by helping them reconnect to theirs.

LEADERS MODEL THE WAY

During the hours and days following the terrorist attacks of September 11, 2001, Mayor Rudy Giuliani gave New Yorkers a picture of how they should act. Six days after the attacks, late-night talk show host David Letterman would say this about the mayor:

> But in this one small measure, if you're like me, and you're watching and you're confused and depressed and irritated and angry and full of grief, and you don't know how to behave, and you're not sure what to do, and you don't really ... because we've never been through this before ... all you had to do at any moment was watch the mayor. Watch how this guy behaved. Watch how this guy conducted himself. Watch what this guy did. Listen to what this guy said. Rudolph Giuliani is the personification of courage.

Like it or not, your direct reports watch you. They notice how you react, how you behave, how you manage change, and how you face obstacles. Especially during times of uncertainty or change, people look to their leaders for cues on how to respond. Models provide a picture for us that we use as a guide. These pictures provide security and comfort and free us to direct our attention toward other matters instead of worrying about how we should respond. In the days after 9/11, people had a picture in Rudy Giuliani of how to act.

A leader's example is also one of the primary sources of trust. People put stock in the values of integrity and honesty and want to see them in their leaders. There is a certain moral standard that is expected from those who lead. When leaders gossip, blame others for their mistakes, refuse to take responsibility, and take credit for success that is not theirs, they lose massive amounts of trust from their staff. However, it's not just their behaviors that are important, but their moods as well. Your emotional state carries more weight than anyone else's on the team. If a coworker has a bad day, the impact on the team is usually minimal. However, everyone knows when the boss is in a bad mood. E-mails are circulated, and word spreads warning everyone to be on guard. Modeling a positive and determined attitude will inspire your team to follow suit.

LIGHTNING ON A STRING

Benjamin Franklin is probably best known as the man who flew a kite in an electrical storm to discover that lightning was in fact electricity. (While Franklin did propose the idea, he probably never carried it out because he would have been fried to death in the process.) What fewer people know is that Benjamin Franklin had an ingenious method for modeling success. At the young age of 20 he outlined 13 virtues he wanted to embody in his life. They were virtues such as humility, sincerity, cleanliness, and generosity. Each week he would choose one of the 13 virtues to focus on, and in so doing he was able to cycle through each of the 13 attributes four times a year.

Benjamin Franklin's list of 13 virtues was powerful because it provided him with a simple system to help guide his behavior. It gave him one virtue a week to devote himself to, and it also helped him stay close to the values that were most important to him. While you don't need to find 13 values, identifying what you stand for and then living it out on a consistent basis sets a powerful example.

Today there is a lot of talk about brands. Companies spend a lot of money to create and promote their brand. Some even go beyond their products, attempting to brand themselves as a certain type of employer in hopes of attracting talented workers. Brands are often rooted in a company's value system. A good question to ask yourself is, "What is your brand as a leader?" In other words, what do you stand for or represent? Just as a company needs to be clear on its mission, vision, and values, so should you as a manager want to be crystal clear on your leadership brand. The truth is that you actually have a brand right now. If I were to gather all your direct reports in a room and ask them what it is like to work for you, their answers would begin to paint a picture of your leadership. The key is not to leave your leadership brand up to chance, but to be purposeful in creating and maintaining it yourself.

Purposeful Modeling

While it is important to be clear about their personal leadership brand, leaders must also realize that different times require different examples. If you are a mountain guide, the way you lead during an easy walk on a glacier will be different from the example you set during a long steep section on an exposed ridge. Leaders must be aware of the changing terrain and adjust their leadership and example accordingly. Be proactive in leading your team members through the various challenges they are facing. For instance, your organization may be going through a time of incredible uncertainty and upheaval with massive job cuts. During times like these, you want to ask yourself, "What qualities do my people need from me now?" The likely answer would be courage, focus, and determination. If you are staring down an unbelievably large deadline that has your team wondering whether or not it can be done, then you probably need to model optimism, determination, and work ethic. Different times call for different models, and a wise leader knows how to discern what is needed when. Your example should not be left to chance; be purposeful. Think about your current terrain and determine what your employees need to see from you this week that will serve as a model for them to follow.

CREATING YOUR AVATAR OR WHAT'S RIGHT FOR YOU

An avatar is a representation you create for yourself. Sometimes athletes use avatars to help improve their performance. A swimmer, for example, may picture herself as a barracuda aggressively slicing through the water, while a football player may see himself as a tank. Such personifications can have a powerful effect on performance. Others may choose real-life heroes as avatars, using them for inspiration and guidance on how they should behave. I have a close friend who found an avatar in a U.S. president. Any time he felt he was facing criticism, he would imagine how this president would handle such a situation. Creating this avatar gave my friend a powerful picture to follow, which provided him with an emotional boost.

A manager who needs to be more aggressive in helping his team reach a certain goal may picture himself as a pit bull terrier, determined to not back down or let go of the target. Managers facing dysfunction and disunity within their team might find an avatar in Abraham Lincoln, asking themselves the question, "What would Lincoln do?" Such scenes may sound silly, but their visual nature serves as a powerful guide to help you consistently model what is needed at the time. There is a reason why some of the world's greatest athletes use avatars to enhance their performance.

For others, an avatar might not resonate as much as a slogan, a motto, or even an inspiring quotation. On many occasions when I have faced the insecurities of venturing into new territory, I have found inspiration in a quote from Ralph Waldo Emerson: "The world makes way for the man who knows where he is going." Harry S Truman, the thirty-third president of the United States, had a sign on his desk that read, "The buck stops here." My father's neurosurgeon had a motto that he used to guide his life. It was even on his business card. It read: "I am responsible for my choices and actions."

Whether it's a slogan, a quote, or an avatar, the important thing is to have a clear picture of what your people need to see in you in order to inspire their performance. Earlier in this book we learned about the principle of weighted relationships and how large a role we play in the lives of our direct reports. Because of this, we want to make sure we lead with passion and excellence, never taking for granted the sacred trust we have been given. When employees have an inspiring model to follow, they will gladly get behind you and follow your lead. Don't leave your example up to chance; be purposeful, be consistent, and use your life to point the way.

MINUTE NINE SUMMARY

Key Lesson

- People look to leaders to know how to act, respond, and sometimes feel.
- Great leaders:
  - Inspire courage
  - Increase energy
  - Elevate performance
  - Model the way
- Be purposeful in what you model.

Key Question

- What model do my people need from me this week?

Key Action Step

- Write a list of the qualities you would like to be known for as a leader.

MINUTE 9

*What model do my people need
from me this week?*

14

The View from Up Here
Why Belief Matters

> *When the best leader's work is done, the people will say:*
> *"We did it ourselves."*
>
> —Lao Tzu

When we finally reached the ridge Osvaldo had marked out for us, there was a mixture of disappointment and relief. I was so tired that I was happy we could now begin our return trip back down the mountain. Yet there was a part of me—at least a tiny voice deep inside—that expressed its disappointment. I had trained for so long, worked so hard, and traveled so far to accomplish this goal, and yet here I was only a few minutes from turning around and retreating in defeat. All kinds of justifications swam through my foggy brain in an attempt to quiet the inner dissent. "It wouldn't be safe." "It's getting late in the day." "We've already climbed three out of four peaks. That's a pretty good success rate." But even with these encouragements from myself, there was still a gnawing disappointment.

We sat longer this time, eating a sandwich and drinking some of our water, which we had been rationing. After a long break, Osvaldo got back on the radio. "Campo Base, Campo Base," he said in Spanish. Six thousand feet below us, someone in base camp responded.

Then, without hesitation, Osvaldo switched to English and told the person on the other end of the radio, "We are going to the summit."

Before my brain could completely register the sudden change in plans, Jim responded emphatically: "WHAT?" as he looked at Osvaldo in disbelief.

"Yes, Jim, the summit is not much farther, just one hour."

"You said we were stopping here!" Jim fired back, clearly agitated.

Over the next two minutes Jim resisted, while Osvaldo insisted. Jim even went so far as to suggest we stake him to the mountain and continue on without him, picking him up on the way back down, an idea I was not fond of, nor was Osvaldo, who responded, "No, Jim, on the mountain we are family, we go up together, or we go down together, but no one is left alone on the mountain."

I remember thinking what a good quote that was but, of course, I had nothing to write it down with. As Jim dug in his heels, Osvaldo relented, saying, "Okay, you see that ridge up there, let's stop there." To which Jim replied, "No, because if we go to that ridge, you're going to trick me and tell me to go to another ridge." As humorous as this seems now, it was a serious conversation on the mountain. Finally, Jim conceded and agreed to give it one last try. I remember the disappointment I felt as I saw my chance at an early retreat slip away. But as sincere as Jim was, he only lasted five or six steps up the next section. It was steep and made even more difficult by deep snow. I will never forget Jim taking charge as he planted his ice axe in the snow. "That's it, I'm calling it. We are going down!"

Jim's mutiny was music to my ears. I asked Osvaldo what our present altitude was. I had a personal goal to climb above 6,000 meters, and I was sure that we had surpassed that. Osvaldo didn't listen to me but instead retreated down the mountain toward Jim. Grabbing Jim by the shoulders, Osvaldo told him he was very strong, and that he could do this. They exchanged more words that I could not hear. I only remember thinking, "Don't listen to him, Jim."

At some point I must have thought all of this was funny because the next thing I knew I was laughing uncontrollably to myself, the way you did back in grade school with your friends when you were trying not to get in trouble. I was definitely feeling the altitude.

Jim then said to Osvaldo, "I'm too tired. I may be able to make it to the top, but I don't think I could get back down." A good point since reaching any summit is only half the goal; real success is making it back down safely. Jim looked up at Osvaldo and asked, "Do you promise that if you get me to the top, you will get me down?"

So there we stood, three people from three different nations, joined together by a short piece of climbing rope, and a goal. With less than 1,000 vertical feet to go, Jim's question cut straight to the real issue. He simply wanted to know, "Can I trust you with my life?" It was powerful, and I waited to see how Osvaldo would reply. Looking straight into his eyes, he simply said, "Yes, Jim. I will get you down." After a slight pause Jim said, "Okay then, let's go!"

As we continued upward reaching false summit after false summit, with me growing more miserable by the minute, something suddenly changed. It was the angle of ascent. While remaining constant for what seemed like hours, it now seemed to be changing, to be leveling out. As I looked up, I saw it—the summit was now in view and only minutes ahead. Driving an ice anchor deep into the snow, we tied our packs to it and made the rest of the way without them. Still moving slowly because of the altitude, we made our final steps up and onto the roof of Bolivia.

It is difficult to describe the experience of standing on a summit. First, there is the view. From Sajama, you can see for hundreds of miles. To the north you see the mountains of Peru; to the west, volcanoes in Chile; and to the east, the Andean chain dividing the high plains from the Amazon basin below. The view is spectacular but seems to have greater depth because of the struggle you have endured to get there. Then comes the realization that you have done it; that you have actually made it to the top and now stand on one of the highest peaks in the western hemisphere. It is a feeling that is hard to put into words; it feels almost scary. Last, there is an amazing bonding that takes place among your teammates as you realize that, without them, you would not be standing where you are. Hugs, pats on the backs, and congratulations are warm and heartfelt.

LEADERS GIVE CREDIT AWAY

While we were standing around taking pictures and shooting some video, I couldn't help reflect back on the last few hours. I felt embarrassment as I thought about my desire to quit and how much I had wanted Jim to go back down so I could return to base camp. While outwardly I had looked like a team player, inwardly I had come up short.

I handed Osvaldo my video camera, and he filmed a minute of Jim and me celebrating. As he rolled the tape, Osvaldo said, "Congratulations, guys, you did it!" With that one simple sentence, he gave all the credit away. The reality, however, was that without his leadership I wouldn't have done it, yet here he was praising us. It was sixth-century Chinese sage Lao Tzu who said, "When the best leader's work is done, the people will say: 'We did it ourselves.'"

The next day back in base camp, I pulled Osvaldo aside and asked him how he did it. I wanted to know how he was able to motivate two exhausted climbers to keep going until we reached the top. He said to me, "I know the mountains. I know that they wear you down here" (pointing to his head) "before they wear you down here" (pointing to his legs). "I knew you were very strong. I just had to keep you going."

Osvaldo could easily have turned us around at 20,000 feet. Whether we reached the top or not made no difference to his pay. He could have simply said that if we didn't want the summit bad enough, there was nothing he could do. But Osvaldo believed in us, even after we had stopped believing in ourselves. When we needed a new strategy, he came up with one. When we needed a small win, he manufactured one. When we needed an emotional boost, he gave pep talks. When we were weary, he adjusted the pace. He did all this because, as a mountain guide, Osvaldo helps people climb mountains. This is leadership.

I wanted to end the book with this story because to me it encapsulates so much of the true core of leadership. People desire to do great things, but, for many, somewhere along the climb they run out of energy. A lot of employees want to believe they can accomplish something great, and leaders help breathe life into them again. We all need people in our lives to believe in us when we ourselves don't, to challenge us

Figure 5
Nine Minutes on Monday

when we won't, and to whisper in our ear, "Just a little farther." This type of leadership is inspiring. As you work on implementing the nine needs that are contained in this book (see Figure 5), you will ignite your team's productivity and engagement. And, as team members stand on their own summit—tired, yet exhilarated, with a sense of accomplishment—you, too, will be able to say, "Congratulations. You did it!"

15

Implementing the Nine Needs

A journey of a thousand miles begins with a single step.

—Lao Tzu

Earlier in the book I introduced you to the concept of "fixed lines." Mountaineers use fixed lines as a safety system in the mountains on sections where a fall would be fatal. For a novice climber, a fixed line is reassuring. Once you reach it, you clip in and then follow.

Nine Minutes on Monday is meant to be a bit like the fixed lines the mountain guides use. By "clipping in," you will slowly and steadily make your way up the mountain of employee excellence. Throughout this book I have outlined the route for you by introducing you to the nine needs which, when met, increase motivation and engagement. Now I want to show you how to use this fixed line to keep you on track as you begin applying what you have learned.

Nine Minutes on Monday hinges on four principles that are essential for any successful change effort. These principles are what make *Nine Minutes on Monday* easy to implement and effective at motivating and engaging your staff.

SIMPLICITY

Earlier in the book, I told you about the work my wife does as a nutritionist. Helping people lose weight is all about replacing bad habits with good ones, and this takes time and energy. When people attempt to change too much at once, the change usually does not last. I have witnessed managers who were sent off to attend a weekend leadership conference only to return to an insanely busy work environment. Because they had very little time, it was next to impossible to implement any long-term change. No matter how well-intentioned and zealous the managers may have been, the conference binder usually ends up on their bookshelf, collecting dust.

One of the keys to change is simplicity. *Nine Minutes on Monday* begins with a simple nine-minute planning time each Monday morning as you begin your work week. During this planning time you ask yourself nine questions, the answers to which will spur you on to create simple, practical action items. Too often people think they need a complex solution for every problem. After speaking at a conference recently on the Nine Minutes on Monday program, a woman approached me and said, "It sounds so simple, I just hope it works." Motivating and engaging your staff is all about meeting these nine needs, but doing so on a consistent basis. There are many complex systems out there to help you lead, but big, bulky initiatives rarely produce long-term change. The key is to keep it simple.

CONSISTENCY

Great leadership is not defined by sporadic heroic events but rather by the little things done consistently. Consistency is powerful. If you don't believe this, then take a trip to the Grand Canyon on your next vacation. The colossal ravine has been etched into the earth by drops of water over thousands of years. One of our challenges today is that we live in an "instant society." We want to see returns on investment in days instead of months. Most of us are willing to try almost anything as long as it fixes the problem by tomorrow. "A new exercise machine to help me lose weight in three minutes a day? How do I pay?"

When it comes to effective leadership, meeting the nine needs on a consistent basis is where the power comes from.

MANAGEABILITY

Any change requires effort and time. The more you are attempting to change, the more energy and time is needed. In today's demanding environment, excess time and energy are hard to come by. I remember as a kid that if there was a hill to climb, my friends and I would begin by running full speed toward it, hoping our cheetah-like speed would propel us to the top. This pace, of course, soon came to an end, halted by gravity and burning lungs. The rest of the way would be made with our tongues hanging out, panting like dogs, and wearily plodding upward. Engaging and motivating employees is not a small hill but rather a mountain, and, as someone once said, "Mountains are climbed one step at a time."

Nine Minutes on Monday is designed specifically to be manageable. For example, we talk about the need for recognition in Chapter 7. The goal is not to recognize all your direct reports each week, but simply to pick one. The rationale here is not to limit what you do—by all means, if you want to recognize each of your employees, that is even better—but the purpose of the simple goals is to make sure that even in hectic weeks, these nine needs still appear on your radar.

HABIT FORMING

Long-term change is the result of building new habits. Aristotle, the great Greek philosopher, said, "We are what we repeatedly do. Excellence is therefore not an act but a habit." *Nine Minutes on Monday* will help you create new habits by repeating the most important practices of effective leadership. These habits will continue to serve you for years to come. The longer you practice and implement these principles, the more natural your leadership will become.

THE NINE-MINUTE PLANNING TIME

First of all, you want to decide when and where you are going to conduct your planning session. You obviously do not need a lot of time, but you do need a place free of distraction. More important than the place, however, is the timing. It is important that your planning session is on the first day of your work week. If possible, try to make it the first thing you do on that morning. This will ensure that it stays a priority and keep it from becoming lost in the shuffle of tasks that eventually will fill up your week. The nine-minute planning time must become a sacred ritual in your week. There are many activities that cry out for your attention, but this is one that you must work hard to protect. The good news is that after a couple of months, this planning time will become part of your regular routine. Until it becomes automatic, however, be sure to set yourself some type of reminder so that when you come into the office on Monday morning, you are prompted to begin your leadership planning session.

Begin with the Big Four

Although there are nine needs, I suggest that for the first month you stick with the first four (care, mastery, recognition, and purpose). The reason for this is that you have time to work on the most important needs before moving on to the remaining five. This two-stage approach is helpful for a couple of reasons. First of all, it helps you narrow your focus on the first four needs until they become second nature to you, before you move on to the rest. Second, this will prevent you from feeling overwhelmed by starting your first week having to think about all nine areas. When you are thinking about some of these areas for the first time, you may notice that some extra work is required. For example, when you think about the need for mastery and the importance of giving feedback, you may realize that all your employees are running on treadmills instead of climbing mountains. It may take some extra thought to tweak their job functions a bit before they are set up for mastery and feedback. When you're working on the big four, ask yourself the following questions:

1. Whom will I show a genuine interest in this week?
2. Whom will I give feedback to?
3. Whom will I recognize?
4. How will I connect purpose to pay for someone?

Drip in the Remaining Five

After you spend a month implementing the first four needs, add one new need each week. This will enable you to add to your skill set at a manageable pace. The goal is long-term habit formation. As slow as this integration may seem, it is an effective strategy for adopting new habits. When you're considering the remaining five needs, ask yourself the following questions:

5. Whom will I help grow this week?
6. Whom will I help feel autonomous?
7. What can I do to foster team unity?
8. Where can I inject some fun?
9. What do I need to model for my team members?

A Nine-Minute Case Study

Nancy the Production Accountant Nancy is a production accountant at a large energy company and has five direct reports working under her. Their jobs are administrative in nature and, because of the routine work, it's sometimes hard for them to feel enthused and engaged in what they do. Nancy conducts her first nine minutes on Monday planning time. Here is what happened.

Because this is Nancy's first time through, she decides to stick with the first four needs. (I love the fact that Nancy listens to my advice.)

1. *Whom will I show a genuine interest in this week?* Nancy likes the concept of the walkabout and realizes that she hardly knows any-

thing about her direct reports. Part of this is the result of her busy schedule and the other is because half of her team is new to the company. Nancy decides to schedule 15 minutes right before lunch on Monday to do a walkabout and learn some of her staff members' vital statistics. By scheduling a walkabout on Monday, it makes it very natural for her to ask people about their weekend. This will help her fill in a lot of those vital statistics.

2. *Whom will I give feedback to?* Nancy has a tough time coming up with feedback for her direct reports. All their stretch goals were created for year end, which is six months away. She finds it difficult to come up with something she could really comment on. Nancy realizes that most of her staff members are on treadmills, and she needs to find them some mountains to climb in order to increase their engagement. She decides to schedule a meeting with her boss to brainstorm some ideas.

3. *Whom will I recognize?* Nancy loves the recognition codes tool she downloaded from www.nineminutesonmonday.com and has decided to use it with Sara. Sara is a new hire who has brought some much needed energy and a positive attitude to the team. Nancy decides to let Sara know how much her positive attitude at last week's meeting affected her and another one of the team members. She puts a reminder in her appointment book to give Sara the recognition at the team meeting on Thursday.

4. *How will I connect purpose to pay for someone?* At first Nancy found this concept difficult. Linking purpose to pay in accounting can sometimes be a challenge. After reviewing the three questions of purpose from Chapter 8, Nancy decides to talk to Lisa about the financial risk report she is working on. The sales and acquisitions department relies heavily on her report in order to make decisions about possible mergers. Without it, the acquisitions department would be partially blind. Her work helps the entire company make better decisions and avoid costly errors. Nancy has never connected

these dots for Lisa and decides that she will do it this week. She plans to drop by Lisa's office on her way to the finance meeting later this afternoon to remind her of how her work impacts the company.

Nancy concludes her leadership planning time with four action items:

1. Spend 15 minutes before lunch today on a walkabout.
2. Set up a meeting with her boss to discuss how to create a more goal-oriented work environment for her employees.
3. Spend 30 seconds at the team meeting on Thursday to give Sara some recognition regarding her positive attitude.
4. Connect purpose to pay for Lisa regarding her report. This will take all of one minute.

Other than the meeting with her boss, which will probably last half an hour, Nancy has made four goals for herself that she can easily achieve, each one taking just a few minutes. They may not seem like much, but they are a fantastic start, and two of her goals will have a lingering impact on two of her employees (Sara and Lisa). Nancy also has given her goals a time and place. This will help ensure that they happen.

Mike the Engineer Mike is an engineer who works for a marine technology company that designs motors for small boats. He has been using the nine minutes on Monday planning time for a few months. By now he has added all nine needs to his planning session. Let's take a look at his planning time.

1. *Whom will I show a genuine interest in this week?* Mike has been enjoying his weekly walkabouts and has learned much about his staff members. Taking more of an interest in them has improved his communication and connection with his team. He has noticed

that even the team meetings seem better. Although Mike usually takes time out every Friday after lunch to do his walkabout, he also knows that Janet, one of his employees, has a mother who is very ill and is undergoing tests at the hospital. Mike realizes that this must be weighing heavily on her and wants to make a special effort to inquire about how she is doing. He plans to talk with Janet this morning before lunch.

2. *Whom will I give feedback to?* Rudy is Mike's newest hire and has been with the firm for only two months. Mike decides to spend a few minutes with Rudy to give him some feedback on the current project Rudy is working on. Mike schedules it for Tuesday before lunch.

3. *Whom will I recognize?* Last week when Janet had to leave unexpectedly to go to the hospital to see her mother, Mike noticed that Steve jumped in to cover her responsibilities in addition to his own. This unprompted behavior is the kind of thing Mike loves to see in his team members. He decides to use the recognition codes to highlight Steve's behavior, linking it to the impact it has on the rest of the team. Mike decides to drop by Steve's office right after his leadership planning time.

4. *How will I connect purpose to pay for someone?* Mike read in the paper this week about a family who had been adrift at sea when the motor on their boat malfunctioned. The family was eventually rescued after spending two days drifting in the open ocean. To answer the question, "Whom do we serve?" Mike plans to share the story at his team meeting on Wednesday to highlight the importance of doing their jobs with excellence, reminding them of all the people counting on them to produce quality engine parts.

5. *Whom will I help grow?* One of Mike's employees, Nathan, shows promise in leadership. Mike decides that he will ask Nathan to lead the project update meeting that takes place on Friday. After the meeting Mike plans to give Nathan feedback on how he did. Mike

is going to send Nathan an e-mail right after his planning time is finished to tell him about the meeting. Nathan will be nervous but also up for the challenge.

6. *Whom will I help feel autonomous?* Mike has already done a lot of work on autonomy in the last few weeks by helping his direct reports have more flexibility in how they carry out their assignments and by seeking input from some of them regarding decisions. Because of this, Mike decides not to set any action items this week in the area of autonomy.

7. *What can I do to foster team unity?* Thinking through the team dynamics, Mike feels pretty good about overall morale, but there is one thing that happened last week that raised a tiny red flag. During Friday's project update meeting there was a heated debate about the best course of action to take on a particular design. One of the team members, Larry, seemed to let his emotions get the better of him and left the meeting on a sour note. Mike decides that this week he will take three minutes and remind everyone that to disagree over design is okay and even necessary at times in order to create something better. The key, however, is not to let it become personal. Being an engineer himself, he knows the challenges that can exist, but wants to remind everyone that they all have the same end goal.

8. *Where can I inject some fun?* Mike feels as though the team has been having a good time lately and sees no need to inject anything new. The team lunch hours have been a blast, and Mike is pleased to see everyone laughing.

9. *What do I need to model for my team members?* In addition to the usual values that Mike tries to model, he sees the need to continue modeling persistence. When Mike took over this project, he noticed that many of the engineers were too quick to get frustrated and came running for help instead of trying to work out their problems on their own. For the last few weeks he has been stressing the need to be gritty in handling work assignments. He has been purposely

modeling it himself by refusing to complain about things around the office and seeking to tackle problems head on. He remembered how Harry S Truman had a sign on his desk that said, "The buck stops here." Two weeks ago Mike made a similar sign out of paper and put it on his own desk. Every one of his direct reports who has been to his office has now heard the story. Mike decides to continue with that emphasis all this week.

Mike concludes his nine-minute planning time with these action items:

1. *Care.* Do a walkabout on Friday afternoon and inquire about Janet's mother before lunch today.
2. *Mastery.* Talk with Rudy before lunch Tuesday to give him feedback on the progress of his project.
3. *Recognition.* Recognize Steve this morning for his initiative regarding Janet's workload last week.
4. *Purpose.* Tell the story during Tuesday's meeting of the family adrift at sea.
5. *Growth.* Send an e-mail to Nathan telling him to lead the project update meeting on Friday. Give him feedback afterward.
6. *Autonomy.* No action item.
7. *Team.* Remind the team at the meeting that conflict is okay but that we can't take it personally.
8. *Fun.* No action item.
9. *Mode.* Take personal ownership, don't give up, and don't complain. ("The buck stops here" motto.)

Mike's planning time resulted in seven action items, most of which take less than a minute. You will also notice that in two areas Mike did not establish any action items at all. Although each action item may seem insignificant on its own, these small continuous steps keep Mike from neglecting his leadership priorities. In times previous, when Mike was busy trying to meet deadlines, he would often neglect his people, burying himself inside his office. Now, even when life gets crazy, he is able to stay out front and in tune with his people.

DON'T SET GOALS WHEN YOU DON'T NEED TO

As you read through the nine needs, you will quickly realize that there are some that you are already practicing. If, for example, you already excel at caring for your employees and the walkabout is something you have been doing on your own for years, then there is not much point in making it one of your action items. The goal is not to create more to-dos, but to help you implement the nine needs of employee excellence. If you already recognize employees each week, then you probably do not need to make it one of your weekly action items.

STACKING NEEDS

Some needs can be stacked on top of one another. For example, let's say that you have been trying to help one of your direct reports meet a need for growth by coaching him in some specific areas. These growth goals might also meet the need for mastery and, by giving feedback on his progress, you are getting him off a treadmill and onto a mountain. Or, in the same scenario, you might recognize or reward him for his progress on his growth goals, or even use it as an opportunity to link his growth progress to purpose.

Such stacking will soon become second nature, but is a good way to combine multiple needs at once.

You will notice that both Mike's and Nancy's planning times were quick and simple. They did not overwhelm themselves with too many tasks that would have created extra stress. I can't emphasize this point enough; effective leadership is doing the little things consistently. Many managers will be tempted to commit to much more. Although this is understandable, it usually backfires. Committing to too much too soon usually sets a manager up with unrealistic expectations. Although the initial enthusiasm might fuel you during the first few weeks, long-term habit formation requires sustained effort over time. Take it slow and trust the process.

CREATING YOUR OWN MOUNTAIN

In Chapter 6 on mastery we discussed the importance of climbing mountains instead of running on treadmills. The key ingredients are clear: optimally challenging goals, combined with consistent and immediate feedback. We also discussed the power of being able to self-measure. Your direct reports are not the only ones who desire mastery. Sometimes leadership can seem like an endless workout on a treadmill. As a manager, it is often hard to know how you are performing in the area of leading your staff. The nine minutes on Monday planning time is a great tool to give you some feedback. Each Monday, your planning time will produce a series of objectives for you to complete during the course of the week. These leadership goals will create a sort of scoreboard that can be used to measure your own performance as a leader. At the end of the week, if you can look at your nine minutes planning sheet and see that you have accomplished the majority of the items, then you should feel a sense of accomplishment regarding your leadership. It is nice to leave the office on Friday knowing that you have done your part in leading your people.

49,740 STEPS TO EXCELLENCE

If Mt. Everest were turned into a staircase, it would have close to 50,000 steps. Add in weather, a lack of oxygen, and difficult terrain, and you have a monumental challenge on your hands. While climbing any mountain can seem daunting, mountains are climbed step by step. Each time you move one foot a few inches ahead of the next, you shorten the distance between your current position and the summit. The challenge with these tiny steps is that they seem so tiny. How can such a little step really make a difference in light of this mountain in front of me? Regardless of how you feel about these tiny steps, it is their small contributions when added together that equal a great achievement. So it is with leadership. Great results are the product of thousands of tiny steps; the same steps I have outlined in this book.

We are often tempted to leave the path when we don't see immediate progress. Quick fixes and shortcuts are not what constitute effective leadership. The route laid out in *Nine Minutes on Monday* will get you to the top, but only by regularly taking the tiny steps laid out for you. At times you may wonder how asking Mary about her son's soccer tournament or helping Joey realize how his job is helping the company actually translates into your team meeting its deadlines. But little by little, and step by step, your leadership will grow in its ability to bring out the best in those around you. And when your people perform at their full potential, the scoreboard will take care of itself and usually in your favor.

NINE MINUTES ON MONDAY RESOURCES

To help you with your Monday morning leadership planning time, download the following free tools:

- 9 Minutes Blank Template
- 9 Minutes Team Tracker
- 9 Minutes Guide

You will find these at www.nineminutesonmonday.com/resources/.

(16)

Nine Minutes on Monday for
Mobile Employees

All things are difficult before they are easy.

—Thomas Fuller

What about managers who are not in the same place as their employees? One such manager might think, "I like the concept of *Nine Minutes on Monday*, but all my employees work off-site. I never see them face to face. Will this work for me?"

Yes, it will, but there are a few things that are important to recognize. *Nine Minutes on Monday* is based on two ideas. The first is that there are consistent needs that, when met, contribute to an employee's engagement and productivity. The second is the *Nine Minutes on Monday* planning time, which is an effective tool to help you address these needs in a manageable fashion. Combining the tool with the practical ideas gives you a powerful system to help you in your leadership. Regardless of whether your employees work down the hall or 1,000 miles away, these principles still apply; however, their practical application may differ when it comes to remote workers. Just as a long-distance relationship has its challenges, so does leading people who work off-site. *Nine Minutes on Monday* can be used effectively with remote employees, provided you make a few adjustments that I discuss below.

CARE

It does not matter whether you work on-site or off. People still want to know that they are more than a number and prefer Grandpa Jack over Big Al, the used car salesman. In fact, one of the downsides of working remotely is the lack of camaraderie that naturally builds in an office environment over time. These relationships are critical when forming bonds of trust. Because you do not see your remote staff on a regular basis, "out of sight, out of mind" is always a danger and can result in feelings of disconnection. This can be further magnified when communication is limited to information sharing only. In a typical office environment you can't help but bump into your direct reports, whether in the lunchroom or the elevator. These small touch points, although seemingly insignificant, do a lot to increase familiarity and add to the daily building of trust. The challenge is to re-create these small touch points in a remote context.

When you speak to your employees only on the phone, or—worse yet—by e-mail, it can seem awkward to inquire about things of a more personal nature, such as how Mary's son's soccer tournament went on the weekend. After all, a call to simply show genuine interest in an employee can come across as a bit weird, unless you have established that pattern early in the relationship. One thing that will help is to make sure that you have a weekly scheduled time with each of your direct reports. Not only is this good for productivity, but it also ensures that you have a regular touch point with each person. If you can accomplish most of your business in 20–25 minutes, then schedule the call for 30 minutes. Having that extra time left over is a perfect chance for you to engage in some small talk and take a genuine interest in your employee. If your calls are only about business all the time, you will fail to build the type of trust required to drive extra engagement.

While it is not possible to conduct a literal walkabout with remote staff, there are some creative ways to fill the gap. One idea is that whenever you have some good news to share, instead of blasting out an e-mail, make individual calls to your direct reports to let each of them know. When you phone people unexpectedly to inform them of good news, it automatically changes the dynamic of the phone call. This gives you a more natural opportunity to switch from sharing good news to inquiring about them.

MASTERY

The principles of mastery and achievement are crucial when you're dealing with remote workers. I mentioned earlier that employees crave feedback and desire to know where they stand. In the absence of feedback, individuals will scan their environment for other cues—perhaps their coworkers—to assess their progress. When people work remotely, they have no one but themselves and whatever feedback comes from their manager to assess their performance. They do not have the advantage of seeing Larry across the hall who may be blazing ahead of them or trailing behind to give them feedback regarding their work.

This is why clear goals and consistent feedback are probably more important for a remote worker than for someone who works in an office environment. Remote workers want you to know that they are working hard, and they want to know where they stand. It is very important that remote workers have all the conditions of flow (clear goals, optimal challenge, and immediate feedback) in their jobs. Each week during your leadership planning time, be sure to outline specific feedback you can give your direct reports so that they know where they stand.

RECOGNITION

Once again, the downside of your dealing with remote employees is your lack of exposure to their daily performance. If they have been working extra hours in order to finish a project, you may never know. It is difficult to know whether they were fantastic with a customer in a phone conversation when you are never within earshot to overhear. Again, it simply takes a little more focus and attention. Remember that people have a need to be valued, and when they are working remotely, the majority of that falls to you. Although much of your recognition will be based on achievements, keep your eyes open for opportunities to recognize both qualities and behaviors. Mobile employees may actually need more recognition because they are lacking the other emotional benefits from working in a functional face-to-face team environment.

PURPOSE

Remote employees face a special challenge in connecting purpose to pay-check. Their separation from the physical organization can hinder their line of sight, robbing them of the satisfaction that comes from seeing how their work contributes to the larger whole. Look for places to link one of the three questions of purpose discussed in Chapter 8 to their role. Also be sure to let them know how their work affects certain individuals at the head office. This can be done by passing on quotes or even testimonials that you glean from other people to pass on to your staff.

GROWTH

Remote or not, employees want to grow. The challenge for remote employees is, "out of sight, out of mind." Everything we discussed in Chapter 10 is relevant to remote workers. Having a clear picture of where each of your direct reports needs to grow in order to be more effective is the essential starting point. Coaching over the phone can have great results. The biggest challenge with helping your remote staff members grow is setting up the process and consistently sticking to it. Remote employees can be trained, coached, and mentored just as easily as those in your office.

AUTONOMY

One of the positive aspects of working remotely is the autonomy and freedom that comes with it. Because of this, autonomy is usually not a problem with your remote direct reports. However, just because people work away from the main office does not mean that they feel a sense of freedom in how they can carry out their role. It is still a good exercise to think through each of your direct reports' job descriptions and see if there is any unnecessary bureaucracy or red tape. Seeking advice from your employees in the field is a way to communicate respect, and pulling them into decision making also increases buy-in and ownership.

CONNECTION

Remote teams pose a special challenge, and one that needs realistic expectations. Trying to build a cohesive team over the phone or the Internet is difficult but not impossible. However, if you do not need your direct reports to interact and work as a team, then you are better off dealing with them individually. Teams make sense only if they have a common purpose. In a situation in which you do need to function as a unified team, the key is to leverage technology and combine it with a consistent structure to give people an opportunity to interact.

Leverage Technology

There are a variety of ways to connect your team virtually. Now that Internet speeds are fast enough to stream live video feeds, it opens up options for you to meet face to face. One manager I spoke with recently attended a regional meeting where other teams from across the country were streamed in. He admitted that the first hour seemed awkward, but then he quickly adapted and felt an unexpected connection with his coworkers who were scattered across the country. What may seem strange at first quickly becomes the norm. Some remote employees who work from home may cringe at the thought of meeting over a webcam. For a few this means changing out of their pajamas or cleaning off their kitchen table, which has been their workspace. Some are worried that their child or one of their dogs may wander into the picture. You can alleviate a lot of these concerns by letting your staff know that it's okay and an expected part of the remote working culture.

Be a Catalyst

While you can't call Bob in Seattle and ask him to take Jerry in San Diego out for lunch, you still can act as a catalyst to get people together. One company I know of had its employees partner up with other remote workers. It was expected that they would speak to each other every week. One manager I talked to initially found this unappealing, but as time went on he realized the benefits of getting to know some of his coworkers. He came to look forward to these phone meetings, which gave him an opportunity to discuss issues or challenges he was facing. This helped build team relationships and took some pressure off the boss as being the only go-to person for each and every challenge.

Face to Face

Of course, the best way to give your remote team a boost is to meet face to face a few times a year. One manager told me that his team members completely changed in connection and feel after they had a chance to meet at the corporate head office. Now he had real faces to picture whenever he spoke with them on the phone or via e-mail.

PLAY

Fun at work is admittedly a challenge in a remote work situation. At the office there are countless moments of spontaneous fun, hilarious mishaps, and unexpected funny moments. Working on your own can seriously cut you off from the party. Fun, as we discussed earlier, is important for many reasons, such as stress reduction, social bonding, and creative thinking. Having fun is something that many remote workers miss once they leave the office environment.

Most fun moments in the workplace usually involve several people. Hearing someone laughing maniacally while she's alone in her cubicle is a bit weird. The best way to incorporate fun is to do it at the team level. This is why regularly connecting your team members is a good idea. When you have a strong team dynamic, there will be more opportunities for fun to naturally evolve. There are creative things you can do as a remote team: office sports pools, competitions of some kind, or carrying on a running joke. The Internet also gives you an unlimited selection of fun material to draw upon. For example, you can appoint someone on your team to find one great joke a week to share at the meeting, or have another member find the best video that highlights stupidity among skateboarders. Fun simply needs a catalyst. If you notice it has been a while since your remote team has had some fun, then possibly have a brainstorm with all of them and discuss ideas on how to lighten up work a bit. It does not all have to land on your shoulders.

MODEL

Working remotely usually means working solo. Whether someone is a road warrior or working from home, having a physical model to follow is typically not possible. But there are other ways to provide a model to follow, and the principles in Chapter 13 still apply. While your direct reports may not be able to see your example day in and day out, they can hear about it. Some suggestions for implementing this follow.

Training

Through training you can highlight a lot of how you think and how you manage yourself. By giving tips and advice on what works for you, it gives team members a picture to help guide their own actions.

Story

By telling your direct reports stories of your own experiences, you are passing on valuable information about what you value and how you operate. People are wired for stories because stories paint a vivid picture in our minds. When you want to draw attention to a certain attribute you need your staff to model, tell a story of how you have demonstrated it in the past. The story becomes the vehicle for delivering the message.

Themes

Providing the team with a theme for the month to guide and direct behavior is a way of setting up a kind of group behavior goal. It gives you a chance to set an example and provides a standard for your direct reports to emulate. Over time, team members will have their own ideas that can then be shared at team meetings to enforce the message.

COMMUNICATION

One last thing I cannot stress enough is the need for proper communication. Probably nothing upsets the apple cart more with remote workers than misinterpreted communication. When human beings communicate, we use a variety of senses to decode the message, such as voice, tone, body language, volume, and the message itself. When communicating via e-mail, we strip out 70 percent of the message and are left with only the words on the screen. Recently a manager told me how one of his direct reports was offended by an e-mail he had sent to her. After a few days stewing about it, she sent back a response asking for clarity. Upon seeing his original e-mail, he was shocked. He had misplaced one word. Instead of saying, "*They* need to pay attention ..." he accidentally wrote, "*You* need to pay attention. . . ." Had he made this mistake while speaking face-to-face with his employee, he would have corrected it on the spot. The other physical cues would have made it obvious that he was not telling *her* to pay more attention but was instead referring to the client. These are the dangers of communicating with remote workers. Whenever possible, try to communicate with your staff on the phone or via webcam as opposed to e-mail. Relaying information strictly with words on the screen leaves too much wiggle room for misinterpretation. Take the extra minute to ensure proper communication, and your remote workers will be happy and thriving.

Remote workers can pose a great challenge to leadership. More care and attention is needed in these situations. On the plus side, there seems to be less interoffice politics and drama to wade through and, with the advances in technology, your remote work team can stay fairly connected. Use the *Nine Minutes on Monday* planning template the same way you would if your staff members were in the same building. Simply make some of the adjustments that have been noted here. Little by little, as you implement the nine needs among your team, you will notice an improvement in morale, engagement, and motivation among your remote staff members.

Notes

CHAPTER 1
P. 8. **What Are You Paid to Do?:** In Ferdinand Fournies's book *Coaching for Improved Work Performance*, Fournies presents a simple and effective approach to help managers shape the behavior of their employees. Ferdinand Fournies, *Coaching for Improved Work Performance*, revised edition, New York: McGraw-Hill, 2000.

CHAPTER 2
P. 12. **Plugging the parking meter:** Leonard Bickman, "The Social Power of a Uniform," *Journal of Applied Psychology*, vol. 4, 1974, pp. 47–61.

P. 13. **Milgram's shock experiment:** Stanley Milgram, *Obedience to Authority*, New York: Harper & Row, 1974.

P. 17. **Your words carry weight:** Maggie Rauch, "Cash and Praise a Powerful Combo," *Incentive* magazine, June 1, 2003: http://www.incentivemag.com/News/Articles/Cash-and-praise-a-powerful-combo/

CHAPTER 4
P. 29. **Eastern Airlines Flight 401:** NTSB report number AAR-73/14, "Eastern Airlines, Inc, L-1011, N310EA, Miami, Florida, December 29, 1972," NTSB, June 14, 1973: http://www.airdisaster.com/reports/ntsb/AAR73-14.pdf.

P. 31. Eastern Airlines Flight 401 voice recording: http://planecrashinfo.com /cvr721229.htm, last words flight recording.

P. 33. Berg Adventures: My expedition to Bolivia was arranged by Berg Adventures, a company based in Canmore, Alberta, run by Wally Berg. Wally is a class act and runs an amazing guiding company. He has an impressive climbing résumé including four successful ascents of Mt. Everest and was the first American to climb Lhotse. Wally's company now takes average Joes like me and helps them reach the tops of the world's seven summits. To climb with Wally, check out his website at www.bergadventures.com.

CHAPTER 5
P. 45. The more trust an employee has in his or her manager: "Beyond the Numbers: A Practical Approach for Individuals, Managers, and Executives," Blessing White employee engagement report, 2011.

P. 45. Behavior not matching: *Managing in an Era of Mistrust: Maritz Poll Reveals Employees Lack Trust in Their Workplace,* Maritz Research, March 2010.

P. 45. We want our leaders to be honest: Jim Kouzes and Barry Posner, *The Leadership Challenge: Volume 229 of J-B Leadership Challenge,* Hoboken, NJ: John Wiley and Sons, 2010.

P. 47. "Caring" the world's #1 engagement driver: Towers and Perrin, global workforce study, 2008, New York.

P. 48. Only 7 percent of employees feel that managers look out for their best interest: *Managing in an Era of Mistrust: Maritz Poll Reveals Employees Lack Trust in Their Workplace,* Maritz Research, March 2010.

CHAPTER 6
P. 62. Motivation hygiene theory: Frederick Herzberg, "One More Time: How Do You Motivate Employees?" *Harvard Business Review,* vol. 65, no. 5, September/October 1987, pp. 109–120.

P. 63. Flow: Every manager should read Csíkszentmihályi's work on motivation and optimal experience. He has some fascinating research on the conditions that engage us. Mihaly Csíkszentmihályi, *Flow: The Psychology of Optimal Experience,* New York: Harper and Row, 1990.

P. 65. Goals elevate performance: E. A. Locke, K. N. Shaw, L. M. Saari, and G. P. Latham, "Goal setting and task performance: 1969–1980," *Psychological Bulletin*, 90(1), 1981, pp. 125–152.

P. 65. The fact that goals result in improved performance is one of the most replicable findings in all psychological research: E. A. Locke, K. N. Shaw, L. M. Saari, and G. P. Latham, "Goal setting and task performance: 1969–1980," *Psychological Bulletin*, 90(1), 1981, pp. 125–152.

P. 66. Over 100 published studies: The biggest boost in performance from goal setting comes when goals are challenging and specific. Over 100 published studies support the fact that challenging and specific goals lead to better performance than do easy goals, no goals, or times in which individuals simply try to "do their best." M. E. Tubbs, "Goal-setting: A meta-analytic examination of the empirical evidence," *Journal of Applied Psychology, 71,* 1986, pp. 474–483; E. A. Locke and G. P. Latham, *A Theory of Goal Setting and Task Performance.* Englewood Cliffs, NJ: Prentice Hall, 1990; A. J. Mento, R. P. Steele, and R. J. Karen, "A meta-analytic study of the effects of goal setting on task performance: 1966–1984," *Organizational Behavior and Human Decision Processes, 39,* 1987, pp. 52–83.

P. 67. Gaps create unpleasant feelings of incongruity which motivate us to act: Miller A. Newell, J. C. Shaw, and H. A. Simon, "Elements of a theory of human problem solving," *Psychological Review, 23,* 1958, pp. 342–343.

P. 68. Figure 2: Anxiety, boredom, and flow diagram, ©Trevor van Gorp. Used with permission.

P. 73. The Three Signs of a Miserable Job: Patrick Lencioni, *A Fable for Managers* (J-B Lencioni Series), San Francisco: Jossey-Bass, 2007.

CHAPTER 7
P. 81. Search and rescue dogs: Julia Layton, "How Search-and-Rescue Dogs Work," HowStuffWorks.com, December 16, 2005.

P. 82. Dopamine's role in recognition and reward: O. Arias-Carrión and E. Pöppel, "Dopamine, Learning and Reward-Seeking Behavior," *Act. Neurobiol. Exp.,* vol. 67, no. 4, 2007, pp. 481–488.

P. 83. Workplace incentives: Gerald H. Graham and Jeanne Unruh, "The Motivational Impact of Nonfinancial Employee Appreciation Practices on Medical Technologists," *Health Care Supervisor*, vol. 8, no. 3, 1990, pp. 9–17.

P. 87. Money makes a lousy reward: Cash incentives study conducted by Scott Jeffrey at the University of Chicago: Scott Jeffrey, Ph.D., "Question the Answer–Money Motivates but Tangibles Drive Performance," *Salesforce Magazine*, 2004, www.recognitionconcepts.com/documents/questiontheanswer1.pdf

P. 88. Cash incentives and car sales: Jack & Colby, 1996; O. C. Schultheiss and J. C. Brunstein, "Goal Imagery: Bridging the Gap Between Implicit Motives and Explicit Goals," *Journal of Personality*, 67, 1999.

P. 88. The majority of cash reward recipients didn't spend the money on anything memorable: Wirthlin Worldwide survey, March 1999.

P. 88. Seventy percent of people felt it would not be justifiable to spend their bonus money on something self-satisfying, like a trip: *Employee Recognition Basics–Employee Recognition 101*, Brimfield, MA: World Incentives, http://www.worldincentives.com/employee_recognition.htm

P. 88. Travel incentives paint pictures in the mind: Jack & Colby, 1996; O. C. Schultheiss and J. C. Brunstein, "Goal Imagery: Bridging the Gap Between Implicit Motives and Explicit Goals," *Journal of Personality*, 67, 1999.

P. 89. Powerful combinations—achievement and recognition: Frederick Herzberg, "One More Time: How Do You Motivate Employees?" *Harvard Business Review*, vol. 65, no. 5, September–October 1987, pp. 109–120.

CHAPTER 8
P. 97. Superhuman strength: Tess Koppelman, "Real Life Superman Saves Young Girl's Life," *Chicago Tribune*, December 18, 2009. http://www.chicagotribune.com/topic/wjw-supermansaveslittegirl,0,4748915.story?track=rss-topicgallery

P. 98. Call center: Adam Grant, "The Significance of Task Significance: Job Performance Effects, Relational Mechanisms, and Boundary Conditions," *Journal of Applied Psychology*, vol. 93, no. 1, January 2008, pp. 108–124.

CHAPTER 9

P. 111. KITA motivators: Frederick Herzberg, "One More Time: How Do You Motivate Employees?" *Harvard Business Review*, vol. 65, no. 5, September–October 1987, pp. 109–120.

P. 112. Intrinsic motivation's effect on persistence: R. M. Ryan, C. M. Frederick, D. Lepes, N. Rubio, and K. M. Sheldon, "Intrinsic motivation and exercise adherence," *International Journal of Sport Psychology*, 28, 1997, pp. 335–354.

P. 112. Intrinsic motivation's effect on creativity: Teresa M. Amabile, *Journal of Personality and Social Psychology*, vol. 48(2), February 1985, pp. 393–399.

P. 112. Intrinsic motivation's effect on conceptual learning: Benware and Deci, 1984; Boggiano, Flink, Shields, Seelbach, and Barrett, 1993; Vansteenkiste, Simons, Lens, Soenens, and Matos, 2005. From J. Reeve, *Understanding Motivation and Emotion*, Hoboken, NJ: John Wiley & Sons, 2002.

P. 112. Intrinsic motivation's effect on well-being: Kasser and Ryan, 1996, 2001. From J. Reeve, *Understanding Motivation and Emotion*, Hoboken, NJ: John Wiley & Sons, 2002.

P. 113. If-then types of rewards diminish performance: Daniel H. Pink, *Drive: The Surprising Truth About What Motivates Us*, New York: Riverhead Hardcover; December 29, 2009.

P. 113. Deci's SOMA puzzles: E. L. Deci, "Effects of Externally Mediated Rewards on Intrinsic Motivation, *Journal of Personality and Social Psychology*, vol. 18, April 1971, pp. 105–115.

P. 115. Stanford prison experiment: A simulation study of the psychology of imprisonment conducted at Stanford University in August 1971, http://www.prisonexp.org/psychology/41

P. 115. Autonomy and sick days: E. A. P. Koningsveld, W. S. Zwinkels, J. C. M. Mossink, X. M. Thie, and M. Abspoel, "Societal Costs of Working Conditions of Employees in 2001," technical report, The Hague: Ministry of Social Affairs and Employment, 2003.

P. 116. Learned helplessness: M. E. P. Seligman and S. F. Maier, "Failure to Escape Traumatic Shock," *Journal of Experimental Psychology*, vol. 74, May 1967, pp. 1–9.

P. 117. **A person who hears why:** Giving a simple reason for a task can increase intrinsic motivation. J. Reeve, *Understanding Motivation and Emotion*, Hoboken, NJ: John Wiley & Sons, 2002.

CHAPTER 10
P. 123. **"Don't Worry About It":** Richard Goldstein, "Kermit Tyler, Player of a Fateful, If Minor, Role in Pearl Harbor Attack, Dies at 96," *New York Times*, February 25, 2010: http://www.nytimes.com/2010/02/26/us/26tyler.html

P. 124. **"Did I grow?":** Towers & Perrin's global workforce study in 2008 found that the second-highest driver of engagement among those surveyed was the opportunity to grow and develop. http://www.towersperrin.com/tp/showhtml.jsp?url=global/publications/gws/key-findings_2.htm

P. 128. **Support and believe in their competence:** Albert Bandura, "Self-Efficacy," in V. S. Ramachaudran (ed.), *Encyclopedia of Human Behavior*, New York: Academic Press, 1994, pp. 71–81.

CHAPTER 11
P. 137. **Team building in Antarctica:** Ernest Shackleton, *South: The Story of Shackleton's 1914-17 Expedition*, London: Century Publishing, [1919].

P. 138. **Our brain is wired for connection:** Stephen J. Bavolek, *The New Scientific Case for Authoritative Community*, Poulsbo WA: Broadway Publications, January 1, 2003.

P. 145. **How to address problem behavior:** Mark Horstman and Mike Auzenne are cofounders of Manager Tools LLC, a management consulting firm. They have a treasure trove of pod casts for managers on their website that are simple, practical, and effective. They have a four-step process for giving feedback similar to what I have provided here. You can find their website at http://manager-tools.com.

P. 149. **How zebras recognize their mothers:** P. Grubb, "Equus burchellii," *Mammalian Species*, 157, 1981, pp. 1–9. American Society of Mammalogists, Northhampton, MA.

P. 150. **Quitting rates of new hires during first year:** The Novations Group, a Boston-based consulting firm, surveyed more than 2,000 human resources and training executives. It found that one-third of employers experience between 10 and 25 percent turnover within the first year. A further one in ten organizations experiences an astounding 50 percent turnover of first-year hires. http://www .management-issues.com/2007/3/9/research/new-hires-seek-a-quick-divorce.asp.

P. 150. **The number-one reason people quit their jobs:** Robert Half International found that more than a third (35 percent) of employees said that unhappiness with management is the main reason people have left their organizations: http://www.hrrecruitingalert.com/3-reasons-new-hires-quit/

P. 152. **The Mitsubishi conference room:** The conference room belongs to the advertising agency Carmichael Lynch, in Minneapolis, MN. They can be reached at Carmichael Lynch, 110 5th St N, Minneapolis, MN 55403.

CHAPTER 12
P. 157. **Pierson Funeral Home:** In 2008 I interviewed Michael Pierson for a segment I was doing on fun at work. He was courteous and professional and yet had some great points concerning why fun at work is critical.

P. 158. **Stress at work:** The American Institute of Stress: http://www.stress.org /topic-workplace.htm?AIS=e71290d736a30bb73a9b88f7dc3d9994

P. 159. **Stress-related injuries:** The American Institute of Stress: http:// www.stress.org/job.htm

P. 159. **Michael Kerr, humor at work expert:** www.mikekerr.com

CHAPTER 13
P. 171. **The Death of a Good Samaritan:** A. G. Sulzberger and Mick Meenan, "Questions surround a delay in help for a dying man," *New York Times*, April 25, 2010: http://www.nytimes.com/2010/04/26/nyregion/26homeless.html

P. 172. **The bystander effect:** David G. Meyers, *Social Psychology* (10th ed.), New York: McGraw-Hill, 2010.

P. 172. **"Oh, my ankle":** J. M. Darley and B. Latané, "Bystander Intervention in Emergencies: Diffusion of Responsibility," *Journal of Personality and Social Psychology,* vol. 8, April 1968, pp. 377–383.

P. 173. **Confidence in today's leaders at an all-time low:** Towers & Watson, global workforce study, 2010: http://www.towerswatson.com/global-workforce-study

P. 174. **Which lines are the same length?**: S. E. Asch, "Effects of Group Pressure upon the Modification and Distortion of Judgment," in H. Guetzkow (ed.), *Groups, Leadership, and Men*, Pittsburgh: Carnegie Press, 1951.

P. 175. **Rosa Parks:** "Civil rights Icon Rosa Parks Dies at 92," CNN, October 25, 2005, retrieved July 4, 2008: http://articles.cnn.com/2005-10-24/us/parks .obit_1_raymond-parks-institute-rosa-parks-civil-rights-act?_s=PM:US

P. 175. **Kitchen Nightmares:** Gordon Ramsey, Fox Network USA.

P. 177. **Rudy Giuliani's courage:** David Letterman's remarks on September 17, 2001, on *Late Night with David Letterman*, CBS.

Acknowledgments

Writing a book and climbing a mountain have a lot in common. They both involve research and a ton of preparation, followed by the long, arduous task of writing, rewriting, correcting, and rewriting again. The entire process is exhausting, at least for me. I have come to the conclusion that writing a book is harder than climbing a mountain.

Just as mountains cannot be climbed alone, this endeavor would never have been completed without the help of my climbing team. First, my wife and three kids have been a constant source of support. I am very fortunate to be short-roped to these four people on this expedition called life. All of you make the journey exciting and unpredictable, and I love you for that.

My mother has acted as my lead guide on this expedition, calling me higher, encouraging me to continue, and correcting mistake after mistake after mistake. She even had to reedit four chapters after losing them mysteriously in cyberspace. Even though I am in my forties, my mother and father continue to be there, urging me on.

My brother, the scientist/manager, also helped out with editing and suggestions. He put up with unrealistic deadlines on final edits in order to wrap this project up.

Finally, thanks to Knox Huston from McGraw-Hill who happened to stumble into my session on Nine Minutes on Monday while I was speaking at a conference. I appreciate your vision for this project.

Index

Bring *Nine Minutes on Monday* to your Workplace

Nine Minutes on Monday is an easy-to-follow system that will keep your managers focused on their most important leadership priorities. The program works because it provides a practical time-sensitive solution to help your managers implement the practices of today's most effective leaders.

The Workshop

The workshop is a fast moving, motivating, and instructional session filled with practical tools and content that managers can implement the very next day. James further enhances the session with video and stories from adventures around the world to make an inspirational learning experience. With over 1,000 presentations under his belt, James knows how to keep your managers engaged for a day of practical training. Your staff will have a lot of fun while they learn the Nine Minute System.

The program comes with the Nine Minutes Workbook, the weekly planning resource, Nine Minute Tracker, blank weekly templates, and access to the online toolkit.

For more details visit www.jamesrobbins.com.

Feedback About James

"James was the top rated speaker at our HR conference."
Mark Hollingsworth—President HRMAM

"Our team left motivated, excited and inspired to 'Reach New Heights' moving forward."
Kraft Foods

"The best leadership seminar I have attended."
Kiro Stojcevski—HR Manager Canadian Tool and Die